101 Lessons

of

Tao

Luke Chan

Benefactor Press
Cincinnati, Ohio

To my grandaunt, Yuk-Ying Fong, for her generosity and kindness.

Acknowledgement:

I thank the ancient Chinese authors and philosophers. Without their knowledge and wisdom, this book could not have been written.

I thank Greg Helmers for featuring the stories in his magazine, *Enlightenments*; Pat Brooks for designing the book cover; Pei-Kwun Wang and Hui-Qi Chen for illustrations; and Jian-Hua Lu for calligraphy.

I thank my editors: Betty Jeans, Dr. Henry Felson, Beth Franks, and John Goodell. In fact, John was more than an editor, he was my assistant (refer to Lesson 13).

I thank my brother, Frank for typesetting and suggestions; Johnny Chin for his ideas.

Finally, I would like to thank my wife, Sunny for her support and insights.

Table of Contents

Introduction

A Reflecting Pond

Introduction

In China, people are taught to respect and follow Tao as a way of life, examples include Tao-de (Tao of virtue), and Tao-li (Tao of reason). For the Chinese, a harmonious, balanced state of yin and yang is close to Tao, even though it is not exactly equal to it, for "Tao that can be named is not real Tao."

The Tao of living is a continuous balancing act. The first step toward achieving a balanced life is to become aware whenever we are out of balance. But how will we know? One way is by looking at ourselves through stories. The ancient Chinese have left us a legacy of short anecdotes regarding the interaction of yin and yang in human behavior. For example, when we are obsessed with wishing for a perfect life, a story reminds us that life is as short as cooking some rice; when we are plagued by inaction, a story reminds us to act now to achieve our goals instead of making empty marks on our boat and waiting idly for it to reach its destination.

Indeed, life is an ever-changing myriad of images. You can view this book as a yin-yang kaleidoscope, with 101 facets on its surface. Reading each story is like looking into a still pond, with one aspect of your life reflected back to you. By recognizing the yins and yangs of your life, you can achieve a balanced state of Tao for optimal living. By knowing that others share your behavior, you can prevent yourself from feeling isolated and taking things too personally, thereby increasing your self-esteem and morale.

Even though the lessons are the same, the stories in this book are not direct translations from ancient texts. Instead, they have been rendered in a more lively and modern style.

When one with the Tao, you are neither too happy nor too sad but always filled with joy.

Part One:

Appearance

外 表

Where Have I Gone

1. Where Have I Gone?

Once a sheriff, while escorting a convicted monk to prison, imprudently got drunk. Noticing that the sheriff had fallen asleep, the monk untied his ropes and freed himself. Before leaving, the monk shaved the sheriff's head and bound him with the ropes.

The next morning when the sheriff woke up, he realized that, instead of the monk, he was the one who was now bound in ropes. After untying himself, the sheriff caressed his bald head and muttered to himself, "Well, if the monk is still here, where have I gone?"

The sheriff fooled himself by assuming that a hairless person had to be a monk. Indeed, it is a human tendency to judge people by their appearance. In this case, the sheriff carried the tendency to an extreme -- judging himself by his own appearance.

Returning a Jewel

2. Returning a Jewel

A jewelry vendor had a rare jewel for sale. In order to attract attention, the vendor displayed the gem inside a jewelry box which was painted with beautiful colors and decorated with expensive looking stones.

"How much are you selling this for?" a customer asked, pointing to the box.

"This is the rarest of all jewels. But for you, my customer, thirteen gold nuggets," the vendor replied.

"I'll pay twelve nuggets," bargained the customer.

"Sold!" the vendor proclaimed. "Lucky you! You have stolen this jewel for only twelve nuggets!"

After receiving his gold nuggets, the vendor turned over the jewel to his customer. The customer, however, took only the jewelry box with him, returning the jewel to the vendor.

Although things that look expensive may not really be so, people usually judge value by appearance. In fact, many merchants wrap their inferior products in expensive packages simply to appeal to the biased judgment of customers. Let the buyer beware!

3. The Mad King

"Our whole country is sad because of our king's illness. How can we cure the madness of our king?" a concerned official asked a group of healers.

"I prescribed the bitterest herb to our king, yet still it didn't help," lamented a herbalist.

"Have you tried lizards' tongues and snakes' gallbladders?" asked the official.

"Thank you for reminding me of these rare medicines, I'll try them on him tomorrow," said the herbalist, bowing.

Then an acupuncturist spoke, "I have put needles on every part of our king's body but he didn't respond."

"But have you used large needles? I mean those as thick as hay stalks?" asked the official.

"No, but I have many such large needles at home and I'll use them on our king tomorrow," replied the acupuncturist.

After the conference these concerned citizens went home to prepare for tomorrow.

The king, however, was the only person in this country who had not drunk from a tainted well. In reality, it wasn't the king, but everyone else, affected by the water, who was truly crazy! Since the king was the only person remaining sober, he was treated for his "madness" every day by his zealous subjects.

The next day when the king saw the huge needles and menacing lizards' tongues, he couldn't face such treatments any longer and volunteered to drink some of the well water. Soon he became just as crazy as everyone else and the entire country returned to joy.

If someone does something very different from other people, he will be labeled either as "talented" or "weird." Have you ever been labelled one way or the other? I have.

Before Tai Chi became more prevalent in the United States, I was often stopped by police while practicing Tai Chi in public parks. Once a policeman waited until I had finished an entire Tai Chi form before approaching me. "Someone called and told us that there was a man doing some strange movements here in the public park. Then when I saw you moving in such a graceful way, I told myself that you couldn't be mad. But are you?"

Today, when I see someone doing something unique, I defer judgment on whether he is talented or mad, for it is very difficult to tell. Sometimes even that person doesn't know for sure!

4. A Beautiful and an Ugly Lady

Once there lived a lady so beautiful that even the geese flying over her head in the sky came down to take a closer look. And every time she went to see her reflection in the water, the fish were so shocked by her beauty that they sank to the bottom.

It was said that she was the most beautiful whenever she grimaced because of a stomachache.

"That's her secret!" exclaimed an ugly rich lady when her servants confirmed that they had witnessed many young men falling to their knees while the beautiful lady grimaced.

So the ugly lady made up her mind to imitate the beautiful girl's success. Every time she saw a young suitor, she distorted her face, mimicking a stomachache. But the more she grimaced the uglier she became.

Meanwhile, no one dared suggest to the rich lady that she should look at herself in the mirror while she grimaced. Soon she became known as the ugly lady with a stomachache, a laughingstock in the town.

Some beautiful women do have stomachaches and grimace, but not all women who have stomach problems are beautiful. So it was absurd for the ugly lady to regard grimacing as a reason for beauty.

Many times we behave just like this ugly lady, mimicking other "successful" persons for traits having nothing to do with success. Once, I asked a college classmate why he had suddenly started pipe smoking. "It's cool and it improves my memory," he replied. Later he admitted that he was following the habit of our "coolest" history professor, one who was known for his extraordinary memory.

5. Wrong Chanting

A high-ranking monk, traveling through a remote village, was attracted to a strong sense of life energy radiating from a small hut. Knowing that only a high-level master could radiate so much life energy during meditation, the monk tiptoed respectfully to the front door and bowed to the master. Through the door he saw a farmer meditating aloud.

"Ha ha ha!" the monk laughed loudly.

The farmer woke up from his deep meditation and was happy to see a high-ranking monk in his hut. Immediately he bowed his head and asked for advice.

"My son," said the monk, "judging by the life energy emanating from this hut, you have reached a very high level of meditation. Yet you have been doing it all wrong. You should say "Healing Qi is Plentiful" not "Healing Qi is Thankful" during meditation. From now on, say the right thing."

The farmer nodded and thanked the monk for generously transmitting this secret.

A few months later, the monk passed through the village again and was surprised to feel no life energy coming from the hut. Looking in the front door, he saw the farmer meditating as seriously as ever and chanting "Healing Qi is Plentiful."

By saying the right words, the farmer had lost his power.

In his own way, the farmer had cultivated a high level of meditation. When he abandoned his old way in order to imitate the "correct" way he ended up powerless.

Likewise, each of us have acquired certain skills in our own way. When we abandon our way of doing things to imitate other "highly successful" persons, we may end up losing our power.

It takes a long time to be what you are. It means something special -- so be yourself!

6. Learning to Walk

Once the king of a weak country gathered his advisors to discuss ways to strengthen the nation.

"My dear advisors, how can we become as strong as our neighboring nation in the North?" asked the king.

"That's easy, my lord," said a flamboyant young scholar. "Our neighbor is strong because it has a strong army. A strong army begins with strong soldiers, and strong soldiers begin with strong legs. Since the strong legs of the northerners are developed by a certain way of walking, if we learn the secret of their walk we can strengthen our nation in no time!"

The king nodded his head because he had indeed heard that the citizens of the North had a powerful way of walking.

"There are no easy answers, my lord," an old councillor cautioned. "Our neighbor does have many strong points which we can adopt, but we must be careful to learn their ways without destroying our own way of life."

The king did not heed the old man's warning and sent a group of children to the North to learn their way of walking.

During the night before the children's return, the king, feeling too anxious to stay at the palace, went to the border and waited to glimpse his citizens' future way of walking.

As dawn broke through the mist the king saw a group of children, one after another, crawling back toward him!

Not only   had the children failed to learn the northerner's advanced style of walking, but they had also forgotten their own!

A nation is strong because of many factors besides powerful walking. If an underdeveloped country forgets its own customs to merely imitate one aspect of an advanced nation, it may end up worse than before.

For instance, many underdeveloped countries have adopted modern technology to their detriment. Where before man and nature coexisted in harmony, now the disappearance of forests and the extinction of species occurs daily as men demand more and more of the earth's space. Without adopting other aspects of advanced nations such as education, resource management and population control, an underdeveloped country is merely crawling on its knees, a victim of famine or tribal warfare.

7. A Bad Leg

"Quit whining, my husband. I am sick and tired of your complaining about your bad leg. From now on, keep it to yourself," shouted the wife of a man who had chronic pain in one leg.

"But my dear wife, it should be *our* business since I am living with this bad leg in this house," the husband replied, somewhat dismayed.

"Then get rid of it!" suggested the wife as she left the house. When she came back she was surprised to find her husband breaking a hole in a wall which adjoined their neighbor's house.

"What do you think you are doing, husband?" asked the wife.

"My dear wife, I have a great idea. If I put my bad leg through this hole to our neighbor's room, it will become their business!" the husband replied.

The wife was speechless.

The husband is absurd in trying to rid himself of a pain by relocating it, but this story is actually addressing our emotional pain. How many times do we, like the husband, ignore the sources of pain?

Don't put your legs away when you feel pain, for it is easier to deal with the source of pain as it happens than to wait until it is internalized.

8. Holding a Hat and Tying a Shoestring

In a remote village, two neighbors were at odds with one another for a long time. Finally, they decided to go to court to settle their differences once and for all.

One neighbor pointed to the other and said, "Honorable judge, ever since I refused to allow my daughter to marry my neighbor's son, he has tried to steal my family's goods. Please send him to prison before he actually robs us of all our crops."

"Can you give me more details?" asked the judge.

"Yes, the other day when he raised his hands to pick plums from our trees, I stopped him just in time," explained the man.

"What have you to say, neighbor?" asked the judge.

"Your honor, I was trying to hold my hat down because there was a sudden gust of wind. This happened just at the time I was under his plum tree. I had no intention of stealing," replied the neighbor.

"But how about the time I caught you bending down to pick our squash?" accused the man.

"My shoestrings had become loose and I was bending down to tighten them when you saw me. I am innocent," pleaded the neighbor.

Since the judge found no evidence of stealing and the neighbor had no previous criminal record, the case was dismissed.

The man in this story created a self-fulfilling prophecy. Because he had disallowed the marriage, he inferred that his neighbor was hostile towards him and consequently discovered many unfriendly acts. Truly, it's quite easy to pile up circumstantial evidence in support of a belief, however, we can also use this principle to our advantage. Simply pick a person in your life whom you have labeled as obnoxious and relabel that person as friendly. Then actually find evidence to support this. Soon, this person will indeed appear friendly.

Tree Shadows

9. Tree Shadows

During a hot summer afternoon, two exhausted travelers took refuge in the shade of a tree. The travelers, a father and his son, moved their positions to follow the tree's shade so as to avoid the sweltering sun and keep cool.

"My son, if you follow my actions, such as cooling yourself in tree shadows, you will grow up just like me -- a smart person!"

The son nodded his head, even though he thought that anyone would naturally seek such protection from the sun.

Father and son resumed their traveling after the day had cooled down. When night fell, the father chose to rest in the tree shadows created by the moon. The son was curious but didn't say anything until his father began to move his sleeping place as the moon moved.

"My father, I can understand why people take rest under tree shadows during the day, but to follow tree shadows at night doesn't make any sense!" the son complained.

"My son, though you might have felt more comfortable under the tree shadows during the day than at night, don't be fooled by your feelings. Use your mind: nobody knows what harmful effects the lights from the heavenly bodies might have on us. So if it is a good thing to stay under the tree shadows during the day, it must also be a good thing to do so at night," the father lectured.

"But, father, isn't it true that the more we move under the tree shadows the more moisture we will absorb from the ground? I am afraid we might catch cold," replied the son.

"What do you know, young man? I have consumed more salt than you have eaten rice. So listen to what I have to say!" commanded the father.

"Yes, father," the son replied dutifully, then murmured to himself, "But I still think it's a stupid thing to do!"

As we grow older and more experienced, our minds may become rigid, causing us to lose our common sense.

Fooling Monkeys

10. Fooling Monkeys

Once there was a monkey trainer who understood the monkey language. When there was a food shortage, this trainer had to carefully ration the monkeys' fruits. He knew that his monkeys would be rebellious upon hearing the bad news, and their anger would be expressed in one form or another.

So the trainer gathered the monkeys together and announced, "Starting tomorrow, each of you will have three pieces of fruit in the morning and four in the evening. Any questions?"

As predicted, the monkeys were very unhappy, jumping around and shaking their heads rebelliously.

"All right, monkeys, I will give you four pieces of fruit in the morning and three in the evening," said the trainer with a sigh. "Are you happy now?"

The monkeys nodded their heads gratefully.

Knowing that the monkeys were thinking more about the pieces of fruit than about the food shortage, the trainer wisely dodged the real issue.

I remember one occasion where my high school math teacher entered our classroom in a huff and complained that the government had promised to give teachers only a two-percent raise in their salaries.

"See, class," our teacher pointed indignantly to the chart he had drawn on the blackboard, "during every salary negotiation, the government always starts at the bottom, causing teachers to be unhappy. But when we threaten to strike they readily raise their offer to five percent or so, and everybody is happy. Class, they have done that too many times! They are treating your teachers like monkeys! Never grow up to be a teacher, class!"

I wish I could have told him that not only teachers but everyone, at one time or another, is treated like a monkey.

11. An Owl Changes Residence

An owl who lived in a forest told a cardinal: "My friend, I cannot find   peace here in the West because everybody hates me. So I am moving my family to the East."

"Unfortunately it's true that you are regarded as a pest here in the West because of your habit of hooting in the middle of the night while everyone is asleep," replied the cardinal. "But Mr. Owl, what makes you think you will be welcomed in the East? Without changing your night habit, I'm afraid you will also be regarded as a pest in your new home."

The owl moved to the East and became a pest there.

Instead of reflecting on why he was a pest, the owl merely changed his residence. By the same token, people often blame teachers for the poor performance of students, government for the existence of poverty, and society in general for its high rate of crime.

Before we blame our problems on others, perhaps we should take a look at our own behavior. Do we treat others as we would like to be treated? Do we have a sense of right and wrong? Are we willing to work hard to achieve our goals?

12. Two "Brave" Men

Two men, both having a high tolerance for pain and a fearlessness towards death, met each other for the first time.

"Although people are afraid of a lot of things, especially pain and death, I, myself, fear nothing. Once I killed a leopard in the forest single-handedly," one of the men boasted.

"I also fear nothing. I once killed a tiger with only my bare hands," the other man bragged.

"I'm glad to have met someone who is as fearless as myself. Let's get some drinks and celebrate," one man suggested. And so they bought plenty of wine.

"I guess we need to fetch some meat to go along with our wine, my equal," one man addressed the other.

"That's right, my fearless friend," the other man replied. "But we don't need to go far to find meat. We have plenty. I can cut some of yours and you can cut some of mine. What do you say, my fearless fellow?"

"Good idea," replied the other man. And so they cut each other up until they both bled to death.

These men subjected themselves to death in the name of bravery. If you think this story is unbelievable, think again.

What about those gun-carrying young gang members, who kill each other as if their lives were worth nothing? Often these gangsters, who are very brave in confronting others with murderous weapons, die young as a direct consequence of their own misplaced courage.

A Carpenter's Hacking Skill

13. A Carpenter's Hacking Skill

In front of a stunned audience, a carpenter raised his hatchet high and chopped a speck of dirt thinner than a housefly's wing from the tip of his assistant's nose. Remarkably, the assistant remained as calm as before, without even the slightest change of countenance.

Years later, a king heard of this incredible performance and summoned the carpenter to his palace.

"Mr. Carpenter, I've heard that you can hack off tiny objects from the tip of someone's nose. Is that true? I would like to see it," the king requested.

"Royal king, it is true that I used to perform such a feat. But my assistant, with whom I always performed, died many years ago." The carpenter replied, with much lamentation.

This story reminds me of something I saw on TV in the late sixties. A kungfu expert, performing live, attempted to break a cement block with his bare hand. Raising his hand, he struck the block hard, yelling, "A Ya!" The cement block fell to the ground unbroken. The martial artist, surprised to find the block harder than he had anticipated, again yelled "A Ya!" and struck the block. This time the block didn't break on impact but, luckily for the martial artist, broke when it hit the ground.

"Does your hand always bleed when you perform?" asked the host when he saw blood on the expert's hand. The martial artist was obviously embarrassed.

That night, instead of the expert's assistant preparing and watching over the cement blocks, someone else had deliberately changed the size and the strength of the cement blocks, making them difficult if not impossible to break! So without his assistant, the martial artist was somewhat vulnerable.

14. Pulling on Seedlings

"My son, I am going to town for a couple of days. Please fertilize the rice seedlings while I am gone; we need to help them grow as quickly as possible," a farmer told his son before he left.

As soon as the farmer arrived home he asked his son if he had taken care of the seedlings.

"Yes, father," the son replied excitedly. "I have pulled on the seedlings to help them grow. You will be surprised how tall they have grown overnight."

The father and son went to the field and found nothing but withered seedlings. Paying no attention to his father, the son lamented, "The seeds must have been bad because they produced weak seedlings."

Fuming with anger, the father took a bundle of the dying young plants from the field and struck his son's head, thundering, "Don't you understand it is not the seeds but your impatience and stupidity?"

Things take time and cannot be rushed.

It is said that one of the sons of the founder of Yang Style Tai Chi, while having the best kungfu skill among his siblings, had no students. He uprooted his students by beating them up before they could master their skill.

Part Two:

Hypocrisy

One More Time

15. One More Time

"All living creatures have an equal right to live freely in this world. So please love them all and kill none," a pious man preached to a group of people. Yet this man was fond of meat, especially turtle meat.

On one occasion a believer offered a turtle for the pious man to release in water. The pious man reassured the believer that the turtle would be freed and that the credit of letting a living thing survive would go to him.

Yes, this turtle-meat lover had indeed promised to release the turtle in water -- hot water. But, being a pious person, the man didn't want to kill. So he put two sticks on top of his kettle, filled it with boiling water, and put the turtle on the sticks, saying, "Now you are free to go."

Realizing that the man was playing a trick on it, the turtle crawled carefully to avoid falling into the boiling water. The careful turtle was utterly exhausted by the time it finally crossed the dangerous bridge.

"Let me see you cross it one more time, you brave little living thing," said the man as he reset the turtle to the beginning position.

Some people can always find ways to justify their real intentions. The man, because he hadn't literally placed the turtle in boiling water, still regarded himself as true to his beliefs.

16. Sacrificing a Goat

After the autumn harvest the king performed the thanksgiving ceremony to Heaven. The king, who had never killed an animal, was a very religious person. When he saw tears in the eyes of the cow waiting to be sacrificed, the king took pity on it and lectured his assistant as follows: "Cows are beings too. We are all children of Heaven! Let it live."

Following the cow's release, the king prayed to Heaven and was quite satisfied with his act of kindness. However, the ceremonial master was dismayed and implored, "Our royal king, if we don't sacrifice a cow, the ceremony can't go on."

"Well," replied the king, "Can't you use a goat?"

The king deluded himself into thinking he was kind to animals by saving one animal while killing another. Such innocent self-deception happens to us all the time.

I once asked a friend, "Why are you still eating so much? I thought you were on a diet."

"Oh, this is diet food, it doesn't count much," she replied, continuing to eat.

17. Eating His Own Words

"Teacher," an old man, walking with a stick, addressed the monk who was the doorkeeper, "is this the entrance to the main temple?" The monk surveyed the old man from head to toe for any sign of dignity. Seeing nothing special about the visitor, the monk held up his head and replied sarcastically, "Are you blind? Can't you see the sign in front of you!"

As the old man was preparing to move on, a rich man in a yellow robe arrived. Wheedling like a dog, the monk said obsequiously, "If you please sir, here is the entrance to the main temple." As the rich man entered, the monk kowtowed repeatedly, smiling from ear to ear.

Observing the difference in attitude shown by the monk toward himself and the rich man, the old man asked, "Teacher, being a holy man, you should respect the rich and the poor alike. Why did you show so much affection for the rich man while scorning me?"

The monk replied pretentiously, "Things are not always what they seem. I bowed to the rich man because I despised him and I ignored you because I respect you."

Hearing his explanation, the old man raised his stick and hit the monk squarely on his hairless head.

"Why did you hit me, old man? Are you crazy?" the monk asked in surprise.

"Things are not always what they seem, teacher. I hit you because I love you!" the old man replied, entering the temple.

Just as some people can always justify their intentions, others justify their actions. Once I read that a thief had hurt himself during a break-in at a grocery store and was sueing the building owner for damages. Why? Because he claimed that the chimney, through which he had entered, was unsafe. The thief was the criminal, but, being caught, cast himself as the victim.

Sometimes I wish I had a stick, and could club such pretenders as I see fit.

Remedy for Curing a Dead Person

18. Remedy for Curing a Dead Person

A healer who possessed a secret family medicine specialized in curing patients with hemiparalysis. Because of the healer's success in saving the lives of many patients, people treated him as a living god.

One day a woman came to see the healer. Perplexed, he said, "I don't see anything wrong with you, ma'am."

"It's not me, doctor. My husband has died! Please save him," begged the woman.

"That's no problem, ma'am. If I can save patients with half their body gone, surely I can save those with their entire body gone," the healer replied confidently, forgetting that he was only human.

"How will you do it?" his assistant asked.

"Easy. I will merely double the dosage prescribed for the half-dead patients."

It's foolish to assume that a drug's effectiveness will increase proportionally when the dosage is doubled. Yet if success is always on your side, it's easy to make such mistakes by forgetting your limitations.

19. Squirrels Know

A man who was fond of animals liked to feed squirrels in the wild. The squirrels came so close to him while feeding that he could have easily caught them.

One day, the man's wife asked him to catch some squirrels for dinner. "How many do you want?" the man asked matter-of-factly. Then, taking some nuts, he went out to feed the squirrels as usual. Strangely, the squirrels refused to come close to the man even though he offered them the same nuts as before.

The squirrels had sensed the malicious intention of the man even though he had tried to mask it.

A person's thoughts are usually reflected in his actions and expressions. Even animals can sense our thoughts.

In fact, some people, understanding that others can feel their intention, actually change their thought patterns. Once I asked a successful salesman the secret of his success. Among other things, he told me, "I concentrate on the benefits of my product to my customers." In other words, a successful salesman hides his intention to sell by concentrating on the needs of others. When customers sense goodwill, they become more willing to buy.

20. A Musical Cook

Once there was a king who was very fond of music. He preferred to listen to orchestral music because he believed that the louder the music the better.

Then one night during an important banquet one of the musicians injured his hand and was unable to play. The conductor, afraid that an empty chair might offend the king, immediately sought a replacement.

While pacing nervously backstage, the conductor heard some staccato noises coming from the kitchen close-by. He rushed into the kitchen where he saw a cook chopping vegetables rapidly with a sharp knife and then cutting beef slowly. An idea came to the conductor and he asked the cook to perform music that night.

"But sir, I am a cook. My father was a cook and his father was also a cook. I was born into a cooking family. Music? It belongs to your family. It is your cup of tea," replied the cook, shaking his head.

"Don't worry, Mr. Cook, the king cannot distinguish between music and cooking," the conductor reassured him.

"What do you mean, sir?" the cook asked.

"The king is only interested in his concubine dancers, not in his musicians. Mr. Cook, when you hear fast music, just move your hands as if you were chopping vegetables; when you hear slower notes, just pretend you are cutting tough beef. As long as you don't make any loud noises, you will be a fine musician!" said the conductor.

The cook followed the conductor's instructions and became a substitute musician for that night and a regular member of the orchestra thereafter by mimicking others and making no loud noises.

Many years passed and the cook continued acting like a real musician, even though he had never acquired the skills. Then one day the king died and his son replaced him. The new king was also a music lover, but with a twist. He liked to listen to the individual performers instead of the entire orchestra. When the musicians took their turns performing in front of the new king, the cook was nowhere to be found, for he had fled overnight.

In large organizations there are always some "cooks-turned-musicians." Do you know one? If one of them is promoted ahead of you because of favoritism, don't be upset, just wait.   Sooner or later he will be discovered and dismissed when there is change at the top.
But, if you are a cook playing along in an orchestra, beware, for you had better learn music in a hurry!

21. A Little Calf

As a man, bound in ropes, was led along a street by two prison guards, another man stopped them and asked, "Why did you bind my friend with ropes?"

"Your friend stole things," replied one of the guards.

"Is that true, my friend?" the prisoner's acquaintance asked with concern.

"Well, when I saw a small rope lying on the ground I picked it up. Some people saw me and arrested me," replied the prisoner.

"They arrested you for taking a small rope?" the friend was astonished at the punishment.

"Well, there was a little calf at the end of the rope," the prisoner admitted softly.

People often rationalize their actions to make themselves feel less guilty.

Once, during a Tai Chi push hands competition, I saw an acquaintance losing badly. I felt really sorry for him and wondered how he would explain such lack of skill to those of his students who had observed the match. The next day I gathered enough courage to ask him about his performance.

"I was the runner-up," my friend replied proudly. Then it dawned on me that there were only two competitors in his division!

I suspect my acquaintance will never be a champion if he continues to rationalize his failures. But who knows? Perhaps one day his opponent won't show up and he will be crowned a champion by default!

22.   A Frog and a Locust

Once as locust was emerging from the ground, it fell
into a pond. In an effort to avoid drowning, the locust
flapped its wings rapidly but could not lift itself out of the
water.

An old frog happened to swim by just then and he took
pity on the helpless locust and carried it to shore. The locust
placed its feet on solid ground then flew into the air.
Swooping down over the old frog it said, "Dear Mr. Frog,
I won't forget your kindness for a hundred years to come!"

The old frog laughed and replied, "You don't even know
winter and spring. How can you remember me for a hundred
years?"

*The frog, being old, did not easily accept empty
promises. As we get older, we too will learn not to take
promises so seriously, especially in relationships. Once a
young man asked his spurned love, "Didn't you say you
would love me forever?"*

*"Yes, I did and I meant it when I said it. But that was
then and this is now," his lost love replied honestly.*

23. Dried Fish

During a lean year, the children of a poor family had little to eat. To save her family, the mother went to a rich family and begged, "Mr. Landlord, we have run out of food. Would you please help us so that we may survive until the harvesting season?"

"Of course, I will help you, ma'am. Your family and mine have been neighbors for centuries. Please come back after the rice harvest and I will loan you as much rice as you want," the landlord promised.

"What will happen to my family in the meantime, Mr. Landlord? Your promise reminds me of a story. Once a fish, whose pond had evaporated, asked a man for some lifesaving water. The man answered, 'Please wait, Mr. Fish, I will ask the ruler of the sea to redirect the river for you.'

"The fish replied angrily, 'I am only asking for a few splashes of water right now. If I have to wait for the river to come, you might just as well see me in the dried-fish shops!'"

The mother left the rich man's house and never went back again.

When we have plenty we don't feel the urgency of those who have nothing to survive on. When people need help, they need it now. A promise to help in the future is an empty pledge.

24. A Chicken Thief

A young thief was caught and charged with stealing. During the hearing, the judge asked, "What have you got to say, young man? Don't you know that stealing chickens is a criminal act?"

The thief begged, "Honorable Judge, even a killer, when he puts down his weapons, can become a Buddha. So have mercy on me."

The judge, pleased to hear such a heartfelt plea, asked, "So you know that stealing is wrong and you want to make amends?"

"Yes, I know it is wrong to steal chickens every day, and I promise, from now on, to steal chickens only once a month. Furthermore, after a year or so, I will steal chickens only once a year."

Upon hearing these words, the judge ordered the thief to be flogged five times.

Stealing is wrong regardless of whether it occurs daily, monthly or annually.

25. Neighbor as a Suspect

After a typhoon had knocked down the wall surrounding a rich family's house, the son advised his father, "Father, if we don't rebuild the wall immediately, I'm afraid that thieves will break into our house."

Meanwhile, an old neighbor also advised the rich man to mend his wall.

A few days later, someone did break into the rich man's house, taking away many valuable belongings.

After the incident, the rich man both praised his son for his prophetic warning and suspected his neighbor of committing the robbery.

Two persons say the same thing, but, because of biased opinion, one is praised while the other is suspected.

People seldom accuse their own family members of wrongdoings. Once a man called the police to report that five pounds of bacon had disappeared overnight from his refrigerator. Under police questioning, his wife finally admitted that she had eaten the bacon as a midnight snack!

26. Monkey Hair

In the netherworld, a monkey pleaded to the ruler, "Great Ruler, please assign me as a human being in my next life. I am sick and tired of being a monkey!"

"Very well then, if that is your wish," the ruler of the netherworld replied. "My assistants, please help our monkey brother to become a human being."

Following the order, two of the ruler's aides held the monkey down while another began to pluck its hair one shaft at a time. It was so painful that the monkey begged them to stop.

The ruler scolded, "If you aren't willing to give up even a shaft of your hair, how can you expect to become a human being?"

This story suggests some rich people, who, each time they give a dollar to the poor, feel like one of their hairs is being plucked.

The story also ridicules people who have dreams or goals but who are unwilling to make the necessary sacrifices in order to achieve them.

Part Three:

Contradiction

27. The Distance of the Sun

On a school yard, a teacher intervened in a bitter dispute between a boy and a girl.

"What's the matter?" the teacher inquired.

"Teacher, is it true that things appear bigger when they are closer to us?" the boy asked.

"That's true," replied the teacher.

"Isn't it obvious that the rising sun is bigger than the midday sun and therefore the sun is closer to us in the morning than in the afternoon?" reasoned the boy. "But she insists that I am wrong!" he added, pointing to the girl.

"Don't be fooled by him, Teacher," replied the girl. "Let me ask you, Teacher, is it true that a burning object is hotter when it is closer to us?"

"That's true," replied the teacher.

"We all know that the sun is hottest in the afternoon. Therefore, the sun is closest to us during that period of time, not at sunrise. So I am right and he is wrong," the girl concluded.

The teacher, truly puzzled, didn't know which student was right.

Have you ever entered into an argument in which you were sure you were right and the other person was wrong?

I've had my share of arguments in life. As I grew older, however, I gradually realized that both parties can be right instead of one party always being right and the other wrong.

On one occasion, I told a group of friends a story about a courageous one-legged bird which was trying to survive in the wild.

"But some species of birds have only one leg," a pretty young girl interrupted.

"Oh, where have you seen such birds?" I asked, muffling my laughter.

"I saw them at the zoo," she replied seriously. I knew she must have seen flamingos, standing on one leg, but just

as I was tempted to argue with her, I realized she might be right. There could be one-legged birds somewhere in the Amazon jungle? -- who knows?

The Quarrel between a Crane and a Clam

28. The Quarrel between a Crane and a Clam

Once a clam on a beach decided to open its shell and enjoy some sunshine. Ever alert, a nearby crane took the opportunity to pick the clam for lunch. But as soon as the crane got its beak inside the clam, the clam closed its shell, trapping the crane. They struggled for a long time with neither the crane nor the clam wanting to let go.

"If it doesn't rain today or tomorrow, there will be a dried clam," the crane warned.

"If I don't let go today or tomorrow, there will be a dead crane," the clam replied.

While they were arguing, a fisherman came by and caught both the crane and the clam for his lunch.

If you are in a bitter fight with someone, beware that a third party may take advantage of your impasse.

A Woolen Hat

29. A Woolen Hat

One hot summer day, a traveler was sweating profusely as a consequence of wearing a woolen hat. When he came under the shade of a tree, he took off his hat and fanned himself with it. While waving his hat, the traveler muttered to himself, "I am very glad that I have worn this hat today!"

The traveler felt miserable because he was wearing a winter hat. But instead of blaming the hat for his misery, he was grateful that it provided him with some relief.

Although the behavior of the man in the story is laughable, many of us act the same way. For example, a woman who stays with an abusive man may therefore become stressed. But instead of removing such a man from her life, the woman is very glad when he occasionally brings her flowers.

30. Unwittingly Aiding Thieves

A petty thief broke into a wealthy house and took away many small items from the cabinets, desks, and other large containers.

Subsequently, when the man of the family was about to take a business trip, he became worried and asked, "How can we prevent thieves from stealing our property, my dear wife?"

"Why don't we tie our containers with ropes so that thieves can't get at the items within," suggested the wife.

"That's a brilliant idea, my dear," the husband replied, and he ordered his servants to tie the containers securely with ropes.

Then one night a group of thieves broke into the house and easily carried away the conveniently-tied containers.

Instead of preventing stealing, the man had unwittingly aided the thieves.

It was once reported that a man complained to the police that someone had broken into his locker and stolen all his belongings. When the police arrived at the scene of the crime, they found that the victim had written the combination lock numbers on the bottom of his lock!

31. A Corpse

After a devastating flood, a poor man found a corpse washed up in his field. Recognizing that the dead person was a member of a rich family living upstream, the poor man sent word to the family that if they wanted the body he would sell it for a large sum of money.

The rich family, not wanting to pay so much for a dead body, sought advice from a wise man.

"Don't worry. You needn't pay too much because the man who found the corpse can't find another buyer for it. Just wait." The wise man thus advised the rich family and charged them a big fee.

When he received no response from the rich family, the poor man became anxious and went to seek advice from the same wise man.

"What's the hurry, my client? The rich family can't get their corpse from anybody else!" The wise man advised the poor man and took a dozen chickens from him for a fee.

Eventually the corpse was eaten by wild animals and nobody gained except the wise man.

In any dispute, usually each party strongly believes that he is right while the other party is wrong. It is often hard to accept the possibility that both can be right.

If you are in a dispute, before you pay a big fee to a wise man, envision the situation from your opponent's point of view. Perhaps a compromise is possible after all.

A Wrong Direction

32. A Wrong Direction

"Where are you going?" a man asked his rich friend when they met on the road.

"I'm going to the Taoist Mountain," replied the friend.

"But my friend, the mountain is in the North, yet you are heading South."

"It doesn't matter because my horses are fast and my carriage conductors are experienced." The friend pointed proudly to his horses and servants.

"But you are going in the wrong direction, my friend. You'll end up farther away from your destination than before," said the man.

"Thank you for you concern, my friend, but please don't worry, I have plenty of money with me for the journey," his friend replied.

"Even though you have plenty of money, you will be exhausted because your journey will be an endless one."

"Don't worry, my friend, I won't be tired because I am young and energetic." And so saying the friend departed.

If a person goes in the wrong direction, regardless of how much money or energy he has, he will recede from his goals.

A friend told me that her father, during his younger days, drank a lot of liquor to catch "inspirations" for his professional writing. Whenever someone advised him that he was ruining his life, he always replied, "I'll quit after I've written some masterpieces." Her father, ever farther away from a successful writing career, gradually lost his mind.

33. Wild Duck

Once two brothers were hunting near their house. As the older brother aimed his bow at a wild duck which was resting on a pond, the younger brother said, "Let's roast this duck."

"No, I would rather deep-fry the duck," replied the elder brother, putting down his bow.

"No, big brother, roasted duck tastes better," the younger brother argued.

"No, little brother, fried duck is the best," his brother insisted.

Finally they went to their father for advice. "You can roast half of the duck and deep-fry the another half," their father suggested. They took their father's advice and went back for their duck. The duck, however, was gone.

Compromise is usually a good way to solve a dispute.
If the brothers had realized sooner that a compromise was possible, they could have successfully killed the duck.

34. The Game of War

During a military strategy class, a student asked, "Teacher, didn't you once tell us that a general ordered his soldiers to dig more fireplaces than necessary?"

"Yes, I did," replied the teacher.

"And now you're telling us that this same general once ordered his soldiers to eliminate more fireplaces than they actually used?" the same student asked.

"That's true, my student. In the first instance, the army was in retreat and in a weak position. So the general ordered his soldiers to create the illusion of a larger army in order to deter his enemies. Obversely, on the other occasion the general had a larger army and, wanting to keep this secret, deliberately eliminated evidence of a large army," the teacher explained.

"That was very tricky," commented another student.

"It was war, my student. War is about life and death -- either you die or your enemies die. A good leader must use tricks during battles," replied the teacher.

"I am an honorable man and when war comes, I won't use tricks!" the student said solemnly.

"Then you belong to the honorably silent group, my honorable student," the teacher replied.

"I want to join that group of soldiers. Where are they?" the student asked.

"Not far, my student, just outside -- in the graveyard!"

No war is just or honorable. In modern warfare, armies may use dummy tanks to create the illusion of a larger army or camouflage military equipment to imply a smaller force.

Often a tricky person will adapt these strategies to daily life, boasting or using intimidation to cover a weak position or lack of ability. Or, by contrast, he will appear humble in order to mask true strength and capability. Let's recognize these strategies when they are employed on us!

Eat in the East, Sleep in the West

35. Eat in the East, Sleep in the West

Once there was a couple who treated their only daughter as a precious jewel, granting her every wish throughout her young life. When the daughter reached maturity the parents discussed marriage with her. The mother said, "My dear daughter, we have received two proposals for your marriage: one is from a man living in the East who is rich but ugly; the other is from a man living in the West who is handsome but poor. Who do you want to marry?"

The father added, "If you are too shy to say it, you can raise your left arm to indicate that you want to marry the rich man from the East, or your right arm to choose the handsome man from the West."

The parents were surprised to see their daughter raise both of her hands. When asked why she raised both, the daughter replied, "I want to eat at the rich man's dinner table and sleep in the handsome man's bed."

The parents shook their heads, knowing that their daughter had a lot to learn about the world she was going to enter.

The young girl was obviously naive. Or was she? She only expressed her wishful thinking about the imperfect world we live in. How many times have you wished you were young and attractive as well as rich?

However, it's one thing to wish you could become an ideal person without flaws, and another thing to truly believe you already are one. If you believe you are a perfect person, you will be in for a rude awakening.

A Drum

36. A Drum

Two men, notorious for their exaggerations, met each other for the first time.

"My family has such a huge drum that, when we hit it, people can hear it loud and clear for hundreds of miles!" one man boasted to the other.

"That's nothing special," the other man replied. "My family had a cow so large that, when it drank water, its head would reach the north end of the river even though it stood on the south end!"

"You're joking, my friend. I've never heard of such a giant cow," refuted the man.

"If there hadn't been such a cow, where did your family obtain the cowhide to cover their drum?" the other replied.

The man was speechless.

Most of us have, at one time or another, exaggerated a story in order to get attention. However, if exaggeration is carried to an extreme, it becomes ludicrous. For example, once during a political meeting, a certain acquaintance of mine presented himself as the president of the Midwest Chinese Society. Naturally, he was very well received by the meeting's organizer due to his prestigious title. Then someone asked him, "How many members does your organization have?" Blushing, he replied, "Two: my wife and me."

37. The Decision Maker

Three men, two clever and one dull, lived in the same house. The two smart men often argued; both of them had their own opinions on everything and would refuse to compromise. The witless man, therefore, frequently was asked to break the tie in their disputes.

The third man, without the intelligence of the other two, had become the decision maker.

Becoming too argumentative is not a clever thing to do. Sometimes it is even outright dangerous. Once in a city on the East Coast it was reported that a woman, on a Mother's Day actually stabbed her own daughter, also a parent, while arguing with her over which of them was a better mother.

Part Four:

Assumption

38. A Blind Person Learns the Sun

A child was born blind and had never seen the sun. On one occasion, the child's mother helped him to understand the shape of the sun by directing him to feel a gong. The child played with the gong for a while and thought that he understood the sun. But then one day, hearing raindrops and sounds of a gong, he asked his mother, "Why is it that the sun is out when it rains?"

"No, my child. There is no sun outside, it's dark," the mother replied. Then she handed him a long candle, saying, "The sun is like this candle, which gives us light." The son carefully touched the candle and thought that he grasped the meaning of the sun.

The next day the child, finding a long-handled key on the floor, shouted to his mother, "I've found a sun! I've found a sun!"

In general, we are poor listeners. We make a lot of assumptions when we hear something, just as if we were blind.

39. Discovering a Man

A rich family gathered their servants to dig a well in their backyard. Everything was going smoothly until the workers struck a rock, and none of them knew how to deal with the problem.

"My son has just come home after finishing his education, what about giving him a try?" the gardener suggested to the husband, the head of the family.

"He is only a child. I can't use him," the husband replied, entering the house in frustration.

The wife then asked the gardener to summon his son. After a while the wife came to her husband and shouted excitedly, "We have found a man! We have found a man!"

Meanwhile, certain neighbors, who were on bad terms with the family, overheard her and immediately went to the sheriff to report that a dead man had been discovered during the digging of a well.

"Where is the dead body?" inquired the sheriff after arriving at the scene.

The wife laughed loudly and replied, "I meant that we had found a capable man, our gardener's son, not a dead man, Mr. Sheriff!"

The sheriff, embarrassed, left hurriedly.

Words can be interpreted variously by different listeners.

One summer during my college years I worked at a golf club as a waiter. Once, as I was giving a customer the glass of water which he had ordered, he began to shake his head strangely and wave his hands up and down. Due to his Texas drawl, I couldn't understand what he wanted. Finally another waiter interpreted for me, "He wants a flyswatter, not a glass of water!"

40. "Hey You!"

A rich man saw a starving man begging for food "Hey, you!" he shouted. The beggar came over and the rich man gave him a piece of meat.

The beggar threw the meat to the ground and said angrily, "My name is Bo, I am starving because I refuse to accept 'Hey you' from anyone." He walked away with his head held high.

Eventually the beggar died of hunger.

To have a backbone is respectable, but a stiff person is easily broken.

When stiff persons are brought to the point of tears because of some tragic event, the notion that "real men never cry" pops up and they walk away from their feelings, denying any emotional outlet. A tough man leads a short life.

When a gangster hears the phrase "You are a chicken!" he reaches for his gun, but if a foreigner with limited knowledge of English hears the same phrase he might reply, "Thank you, sir. I didn't know I was delicious!" Words mean different things to different people.

So be aware, each time your blood runs hot from hearing some rude words, lest you become a starving beggar.

41. Three Persons Make a Tiger Real

Once a king told his most trusted advisor, "My loyal friend, I am sending you as my representative to our neighboring king's birthday celebration. Please return as soon as possible because I need you here."

The advisor knew that, surrounding the king, there were many officials with ambitions to replace him who would seize any opportunity to do so in his absence. Since the advisor did not dare talk to the king directly about his concern, he hinted at it by asking, "Royal King, if someone told you there was a tiger on the street, would you believe him?"

"No, I wouldn't," replied the king.

"If a second person told you about the tiger on the street, would you believe him?" the advisor continued.

"No, I wouldn't," the king repeated.

"What if a third person told you the same thing, would you believe him?"

After pondering for a while, the king replied, "Yes, I would believe him."

"As you see, Royal King, in the absence of any concrete evidence, it would take the statements of three persons to make you accept a false report as true. Since there are more than three persons in your court, Royal King, beware of what you will hear while I am gone." With that, the advisor reluctantly left on his trip.

Upon returning to the palace, the advisor found he had been replaced and that the king did not wish to see him.

People tend to weigh negative criticism more heavily than positive criticism. For instance, a beautiful woman may devalue her entire appearance because a few people have casually pointed out a flaw on her nose or a tiny scar on her cheek. As a result, she may feel uncomfortable around people, being preoccupied with her small imperfection and her wish to hide it.

To balance our natural tendency toward negativity, we should emphasize our positive thinking. If you are down, remember the times when you were feeling great; if you are sick, affirm that you are healthy; if you are stressed, visualize yourself on vacation.

42. Buying a Pair of Shoes

Once a man went to a marketplace to buy a pair of shoes. However, when a vendor handed him a pair of shoes to try on, the man couldn't find the piece of paper on which he had written his foot size. So he told the vendor, "I forgot my foot size but I will go home to get it and be back soon. Please hold this pair of shoes for me."

"Why don't you just try those shoes on your feet, sir?" the vendor suggested.

"No, I don't trust my feet," replied the man, hurrying away.

The man had no imagination: he only knew that a foot measurement was needed in order to buy a pair of shoes. He didn't trust himself when the situation called for a change of plan.

Similarly, many of us can't change and always stick to an old way. I once gave a ride to a salesclerk who worked in a store I frequently visited. The trip should have taken ten minutes but it actually took more than a half hour because she insisted I follow the bus route -- the only way she knew!

43. Humble Advice

A farmer, carrying a long bamboo pole, stopped in front of the entrance to a city. However, the opening in the gate wasn't wide enough to allow the farmer to carry his pole horizontally, nor high enough vertically. While the farmer was thinking of a way to enter the city, a man approached to advise him: "Mr. Farmer, I am not a learned man, but I believe if you cut the bamboo pole in half, you can enter the city without any problem."

Normally the farmer would have thought carefully about taking any wiseman's advice. However, because the man had humbled himself by admitting he was not a scholar, the farmer took his foolish advice.

Is it hard to believe that someone would take such bad advice? When I first came to the United States, I too accepted absurdly bad advice. For example, a college classmate of mine once showed me a list of names and told me that if I would merely give fifty dollars to himself and to the first name on the list, I could eliminate the first name on the list and put my name down as the tenth. Then if I could persuade my friends, who in turn would persuade their friends, my name would eventually appear at the top, and soon I would be receiving thousands of dollars!

While I was pondering this "too-good-to-be-true" offer, my classmate said humbly, "I am not a world traveler and I don't know much about other countries, but here in the U.S. many people become rich because they take chances."

His humble nature convinced me, so I gave him fifty dollars and sent fifty dollars to the first name on the list. Unwittingly, I became a victim of a pyramid scheme and lost one hundred much-needed dollars.

44. Twin Girls

A widower raised his twin girls to maturity after their mother died. The father was very protective of his daughters, and never allowed them to venture forth in public. He taught them to be modest and humble, for he himself was a very humble man.

When people asked about his daughters the widower always answered, "My ugly daughters are fine, thank you." By debasing his daughters, he thought people would feel good about their own. Because he had always described his daughters as ugly, people began to believe his words. If it wasn't true, why didn't he let his daughters go out to see the beautiful flowers in the springtime and colorful leaves in the fall?

When suitors approached the father seeking to marry his daughters, he always said humbly, "Though my daughters were raised properly, they are not great beauties, and if you don't mind, I would be more than happy to let you have one of them." However, all of the suitors were scared away by such tactics and his daughters remained unmarried.

Then one day a poor scholar, who needed a place to live, proposed to the girls. The father said humbly, "Nobody so far has been interested in my daughters. If you want to marry one, you are welcome to." Out of necessity, the poor scholar took the hand of one of the daughters.

On their wedding night, the groom, fearful that his bride might be a monster with only one ear or no mouth, hesitated to get close to her. After waiting for a long while, the bride asked, "I heard that when people get married, as soon as they are alone, the husband always lifts his wife's veil. Why are you not opening my veil? Don't you like me?"

Finally the groom, with his eyes closed, lifted the bride's veil. But when he slowly opened his eyes, his mouth dropped instantly. Instead of the ugly girl suggested by his father-in-law, he saw a beautiful maiden with a gracious smile and sparkling eyes. He touched her face and found it as smooth as that of a baby. He could not contain his excitement and fainted.

The next day, the happy groom told his friend about his good fortune. His friend immediately asked for the hand of the other daughter and found she was just as beautiful as her twin.

Although modesty is desirable, being too humble is detrimental to oneself and to others. If we habitually belittle ourselves in front of others, very soon people will assume that we actually are incompetent.

45. Lost A Hoe

While working in a field, a farmer heard his dog barking fiercely back at home. He quickly returned to his house to see if someone was trying to break in. No one was there and the farmer was relieved. In the meantime, his wife had also come home upon hearing the dog bark, and after inspecting their farming tools, she shouted, "Where is our brand new hoe?"

"It's in the field!" the husband shouted back.

"Shhh," said the wife softly, putting her finger on her lips. "Don't shout, someone might hear. Now please go and fetch the hoe."

When the wife saw her husband coming home empty-handed, she asked loudly, "Where is our hoe?"

The farmer put his finger on his lips, and coming near to his wife, said quietly, "It has disappeared."

The farmer represents an extreme case of a person who cannot differentiate between what is confidential and what is not. But haven't we all occasionally said aloud something which we shouldn't have?

There is a time to speak loudly and a time to whisper.

46. Battle of the Mind

A general received news that an opposing army had abandoned its capital so he immediately marched his army toward the enemy city. When the general reached the outskirts he saw the main entrance to the city was wide open; a few old soldiers were sweeping the floor, oblivious to the oncoming slaughter. The general, suspecting that his opposing army was luring him into the city, ordered an immediate retreat.

In the city, the prince saw his enemies had left, and sighed with relief. But just as he was about to take a much-needed rest, a flamboyant assistant rushed in and announced, "Royal Prince, I have destroyed the bridge along the enemy's retreating route. This will make their retreat more difficult!"

Upon hearing the report, the prince's face turned ashen. He understood that once the enemy general saw a broken bridge but no pursuing army, he would easily deduce that the city was indeed empty and return to conquer it.

The prince, pacing for a while, came up with an idea. He ordered many common people to dress as soldiers and stand on the rampart. Then he directed all available horse carriages in the city to be bound with tree branches and circled along dusty roads in the direction where his defending army would have entered the city.

As expected, the general returned with his army. But when he saw many soldiers on the city fort and dust filling the sky, he concluded the defending army had returned. The general fled -- his army discarding a lot of equipment and supplies in its panicked retreat.

The general, overly suspicious in nature, was played a fool by the prince. Sometimes we need to trust our "gut" feelings instead of our logical deductions based on many assumptions.

47. Strong Words Defy Reason

There once lived a carpenter who was a skillful worker but a poor communicator. He was hired by a rich man to build a new house; the rich man also asked his nephew, a good debater, to supervise the construction of his house.

Everything went smoothly until the lumber arrived.

"Sir, I recommend that we stop our work for now until the lumber dries," the carpenter said. "If we use this wet lumber to build the house, it won't be stable."

"So lumber is stronger when dried than when wet, is that right?" asked the nephew.

The carpenter hesitated because he wasn't sure.

"Is that right?" repeated the nephew.

Finally, since he had always built his houses with dried lumber, the carpenter replied, "That's right."

"Thank you," the nephew continued. "I guess the cement, which we are going to use for the roof, is heavier when wet than when dried?"

"Obviously, sir," agreed the carpenter.

"In your area of expertise, good carpenter, do you think this wet lumber can support a wet roof, even temporarily?"

"Yes, of course, sir," the carpenter replied.

"Then tell me, good carpenter, if wet lumber can hold up heavy cement, won't it be much more effective when it dries and the cement becomes lighter? Isn't it a strong house that we all want to build?"

"Yes, sir, we want to build a strong house."

"Then what are we waiting for?"

So without waiting for the lumber to dry, the carpenter went forward and completed the house. Thus built, the house collapsed a few months later during a mild storm.

Even though we have logical minds they don't always function logically. The nephew thought that a house built with wet lumber must be a strong one. He failed to consider how the house would be damaged when the lumber dried and shrank.

When someone continuously asks you questions which have simple yes or no answers, beware, for this person might be using faulty logic on you. Dishonest salesmen often use this tactic to entice customers into buying. Once a customer drove his newly purchased used car to his used car salesman and asked, "Sir, would you please tell me again all the good things about this car? I have gotten so discouraged." Let the buyer beware!

Part Five:

Self-Deception

48. Stealing a Bell

A golden bell hung on the front door of a wealthy house, suspended in such a way that it rang loudly and clearly even if someone only tapped on the door. Day and night, there was always a guard stationed within hearing distance of the bell.

One day the bell rang continuously as if someone was pounding nonstop at the door. The servants rushed to the front door to investigate the source of this unusual disturbance. They were amazed to find a thief climbing cautiously up a ladder towards the golden bell, totally oblivious to the commotion around him. Then they noticed that the thief was muffling his ears with his hands. When caught, the thief appeared surprised and asked, "How did you know I was here, since I made no noise whatsoever?"

All the servants laughed.

In this story, the thief's hands blocked his hearing, rendering him deaf and cutting him off from the real world. In our lives, there are many invisible hands blocking our judgment. Some people drink excessive amounts of alcohol or take drugs to numb their senses. Unfortunately, when they wake up "the bell is still ringing."

49. A White Pig

"Miracle! Miracle!" exclaimed a farmer when he found his black pig had given birth to a white suckling. In the remote area where the farmer lived, pigs had either black or gray skin, never white. Since the farmer had never seen or heard of white pigs, he thought this pig would make a great gift to the king in the North. So he bound the pig in an oxen cart, bade his wife goodbye and traveled to the North.

When the farmer came home unexpectedly with his white pig, his wife asked him anxiously, "What happened, my dear husband? Why have you come home so soon?"

"What would you have done, my dear wife, if you saw white pigs running everywhere on your way to the king?" the embarrassed farmer replied.

When you have developed some skill and think it is unique, think again, for it maybe as common as "white pigs."

On the other hand, if you have a problem and think you are the only one in the world having this problem, look around, you will find many people with similar "white pigs."

50. A Bird's Feast

A rare and beautiful seabird, having lost its sense of direction, flew into a temple for a rest. Someone caught the bird and presented it to the king.

Seeing such a magnificent bird for the first time, the king ordered the best meat, the oldest wine, and the most beautiful music for the bird's enjoyment. However, the bird refused to eat and starved to death after three days. The king lamented, "What a stubborn bird! I treated him just like I treat myself and it still chose to die."

Meanwhile, no one dared tell the king that the bird did not eat meat, drink wine, or listen to music. The king, thinking only of himself, had loved the bird to death.

If we think only of our own interests all the time, we will limit our opportunities.

During the late seventies, when China began to open its doors to the West, the Chinese people were largely unacquainted with the outside world. On one occasion, an American businessman told his Chinese host, "I am inviting some friends over for a banquet. Please spare no expense in preparing the finest meal you can." Ignorant of American tastes, the host prepared a feast after the fashion of the ancient Chinese Emperors. The menu contained such exotic items as swallow's saliva soup; the webs and tongues of ducks; and the tendrils of carp. Would you prefer such a feast to a hamburger? Ignorant of the tastes of his guests, the Chinese host almost starved them to death with expensive food.

51. A Watchdog

A man was very fond of his watchdog, for its ferociousness had kept away all intruders.

Unfortunately, this dog also had a habit of urinating into the same well from which his owner obtained drinking water. Many times a neighbor tried to warn the dog owner of this mischief, but each time the neighbor attempted to approach the house he was chased away by the dog.

So, without outside information, the dog owner continued to love his dog and drink its urine.

This story reminds us that relying on one person alone for protection or information is not healthy. Such a person, acting as a "watchdog," can easily manipulate our agenda and isolate us from the real world.

Invisible Man

52. Invisible Man

Once a man heard that if one tried hard enough in any particular endeavor one would always succeed. After pondering for a long time, the man concluded that he had discovered a method that would eventually enable him to become invisible. He took a leaf from a tree in his backyard and covered one of his eyes with it.

"Everyday I will imagine I am becoming smaller and smaller. One day I will be as tiny as this leaf and nobody will see me," the man affirmed.

After a few days the man went to his wife and asked, "My dear wife, can you see me?"

"Surely, why?" his wife replied.

Then the man held a leaf to cover his left eye and asked again, "Wife, can you see me now?"

"Of course, my husband. What is this game you are playing?" laughed his wife.

The man didn't answer and left, murmuring to himself, "Persistence, persistence."

After a few days the man asked his wife again. The answer was still the same. The man grew more and more anxious, and pestered his wife every day with the same question. Finally the wife became so irritated that she answered, "No, I can't see you now!" The man, thinking that he had finally obtained invisibility, became ecstatic. Immediately he went to the marketplace, and holding a leaf in front of one of his eyes, tried to steal goods from the vendors. When caught, he asked incredulously, "How can you people see me?" All the vendors and spectators laughed.

If we reinforce some idea over and over again, the idea, no matter how fantastic, will become a reality in our minds. Perhaps it is time for us to take off our "leaves" and look at ourselves from the viewpoint of others. Subsequently, we will realize that how we perceive ourselves is quite different from how others perceive us.

53. A Fifty Step Laughed at a Hundred Step

"Why are you laughing, soldier?" asked a scholar as he encountered a soldier running from a battlefield.

"Look at that coward escaping from the fighting," said the soldier, pointing to another renegade running ahead of him.

"So you have escaped fifty steps from the front and are laughing at another soldier who has escaped one hundred steps?" the scholar asked incredulously.

"That's right, sir. He is a real coward," replied the soldier, running on.

It is easier to see others' faults than those of our own. A fool will criticize people's shortcomings while a wise man will reflect on his own flaws and learn from them.

54 A Dreamer's Talk

One morning the son of a wealthy landlord became confused between his dreams and reality. When he saw the maid, he asked, "Do you remember seeing me last night?"

"No, I was in my room last night and my mother can testify to that," replied the young maid.

"Don't deny it! I saw you in my dream last night." The young landlord insisted and, being a spoiled child, went to his father saying, "We should punish the maid because she denied her appearance in my dream."

"But my son, it was only a dream," replied his father.

"How do you know, my father? Even as we speak, we might be in a dream. Will you deny that I am talking to you now?" the son argued.

The father was dismayed at his son's logical madness.

A crazy person may seem logical. Once when I was unemployed, I engaged in a conversation with an older man in a Dunkin' Donuts coffee shop. When he asked me what I did for a living I told him I had been doing accounting. Knowing I was desperate for work, he showed me some business documents and then invited me to do his companies' bookkeeping. In addition, to show off his wealth, he flashed in front of me many revealing pictures and letters from gorgeous women. Before he left, he even asked me to help him to find a local office so he could relocate his many companies.

The next day I accompanied him to an office leasing company he had visited once before and introduced me as his personal accountant to the leasing agent. While the man was away for a few moments I talked to the agent about this strange man. She mentioned that she had felt uneasy about the man at first but now that he'd come back with an accountant, she regarded him more favorably.

When I got home I phoned a friend whose opinion I respected, and invited him to meet this man the next day at "company documents," he asked me to leave immediately. The papers, even though neatly typed, were nonsense.

"So I didn't read those papers, but what about his beautiful mistresses? If he isn't for real, how can he afford them?" I asked, still not sure.

"You can buy as many sleazy pictures and hot letters as you want by responding to personal ads in trashy magazines," my friend replied. My face turned red as I realized that I had been fooled by a logical madman.

55. The King's Bow

One day a king who loved archery was showing off his strength to his generals. With all his might the king raised his bow and opened it to its fullest. All the generals clapped their hands and praised him.

"Let me try it," asked one of the generals, known for his flattery. Grimacing, the general opened the bow halfway and pretended he couldn't go on, declaring the strength of this bow was at a nine-degree level. In fact, the strength of the bow was no more than three degrees.

The rest of the generals followed suit, all pretending that they couldn't open the bow to its fullest and agreeing that the bow's strength was at least nine degrees. The king was pleased.

So all his life the king believed his bow to be at a nine-degree level even though in reality it had only the strength of three degrees.

We often falsely perceive our own abilities. This is especially true of rich and famous people who sometimes receive so much flattery that they end up living entirely in a fantasy world. Yet others, because of excessive criticism, live in a tortured world of continuous self-doubt.

To have a truly realistic view of our own abilities, we should learn to look at ourselves objectively instead of relying too much on the words of others.

Dancing Wild Chicken

56. Dancing Wild Chicken

A long time ago in the southern mountains there lived a species of wild chicken that loved to dance above the surface of water while admiring its own beautiful feathers.

A king in the North received one such beautiful bird as a present. But though he tempted it with the best chicken feed, the king couldn't make the chicken dance. Even when he threatened it with a stick, the chicken remained dull, merely standing in its cage, staring into the air.

Then one of the king's advisors who knew the behavior of this type of chicken brought in a large mirror and placed it in front of the bird. When the chicken saw its own image, it began to dance admirably!

Some people, like the chicken, are so vainglorious that they only worship their own images, falsely regarding themselves as all-important persons.

Our mind is a mirror. If we keep our ideas to ourselves, dancing with them only in front of our mind's mirror, we will have limited success in life. It is only by freely sharing our ideas with others that we can become better dancers!

57. Don't Hit the Dog!

A man who had come to visit his brother for a few days
went out one morning wearing a white coat. It rained while
he was out, so he changed his white coat to a black one
before returning to his brother's house. Upon the visitor's
return, the house dog barked ferociously because it couldn't
recognize the guest. Angry at the dog's unfriendliness, the
visitor picked up a stick in order to strike it.

"My dear brother, please don't hit the dog. What if a
dog with white hair had gone out in the morning and
returned with dark hair in the evening -- would you have
recognized it?" his brother pleaded.

Looking at his black coat, the visitor laughed and put
down the stick.

*In most cases when people criticize us they have a
reason, just as the dog barking at the visitor had its reason.
So instead of getting upset and hitting back, maybe it's wiser
to view ourselves from the angle of our critics. Consequently,
we may even learn something from them.*

Part Six:

Learning

Mastery

58. Mastery

A master was teaching his student archery in an open field. After the student had almost hit his target with his arrows, he asked, "Master, have I mastered the art of archery?"

"How could you have mastered the art if you can't even hit the target?" the teacher asked. The student realized he had a long way to go before becoming a master.

Two years later, again the student asked his teacher if he had attained the art of archery. This time he actually had hit the target with his arrows.

"Do you know how you hit the target?" asked the master.

"I don't know. I just did it," the student replied.

"Then you haven't mastered your skill. Go home and train more!"

Three years later, the student as his teacher watched, again raised his bow and hit the target easily. He then asked, "Master, now do you think I have mastered the skill of archery?" .

"Do you know how you hit the target?"

"Yes, I do, Master!" the student replied proudly.

The teacher nodded with approval.

Merely being able to do a certain thing is not enough to qualify someone as a master. Without knowing the underlying principles of how a something is done, we cannot accomplish the same thing in a consistent manner. In other words, true masters employ not just their bodies, but also their minds.

Once a teacher corrected the grammatical mistake of her student, Michael, by asking him to write one hundred times the sentence "I have gone." When Michael had dutifully finished his sentences he left the classroom, writing on the blackboard "I have went, Michael."

59. Falling Down

A man fell down on the street and as soon as he got up he fell down again. The man murmured to himself, "If I had known I would fall the second time, I wouldn't have gotten up the first time."

One may fall many times before finally getting on one's feet. If we are afraid of failure we will never succeed.

60. Killing a Pig to Teach a Child

Once a mother told her young child, "My son, I am going to town on some business, and so must leave you home with your father."

"No, I want to go with you, Mother," the child begged.

"Sorry my son, but my trip is strictly adult business. You must to stay home." The mother was adamant.

"I want to go! I want to go!" the child cried.

To pacify her son, the mother promised, "If you behave yourself, I will kill a pig for our dinner when I come home." The child was satisfied and the mother left for town.

When the mother came home she was surprised to see her husband ready to kill a pig.

"My dear husband, I was only teasing when I told our son that we were going to kill a pig for dinner. We can't afford to lose our pig."

"My dear wife, teaching a child is not a teasing matter. You have promised our son pork chops for dinner and he is relying on your promise. If you don't carry through with your word how will he learn to keep his promises? I would rather sacrifice our pig than our child." With that, the husband proceeded to kill the pig.

What we learn in childhood greatly affects our lives. Some years ago, I ran a small business and had a secretary who was a hard working, sensible and caring individual. I was surprised when she told me her father had abused her and that she had run away from home at a very young age. "This is the first formal job I've had. I'm grateful for this job," she told me. Likewise, I was happy to have such a competent secretary.

Then one day she came in with a bruised eye and told me her live-in boyfriend had hit her. "Every time he gets drunk, he loses control of himself. But I love him and want to marry him," she added. Despite the abuse, marry him she did. Last I heard, she had two kids and was living on welfare.

My secretary, even though intelligent and caring, couldn't disentangle herself from the net her father had thrown over her during childhood.

61. Candlelight

"Let's go fishing!" shouted a neighborhood boy as he walked into his classmate's room.

"Shhh," whispered the classmate, pointing to the wall, "My father is studying in next room and his father in the next. Let's be quiet."

When they were out in the courtyard, the neighborhood boy raised his hands and shouted, "It's a beautiful day. We'll catch lots of fish!"

"Shhh," whispered his classmate, putting his finger to his lips, "My great-grandfather is studying upstairs, he can hear us."

The neighborhood boy restrained his laughter until they were out on the road, then said, "I can't understand it. When will your family ever quit learning? Do your grandfather and his father want to take their knowledge to their graves?"

His classmate, who was brought up in a gentle way, replied, "To the young, learning is like the sunrise; to the middle-aged, like the midday sun; to the old, like the sunset; and, to the very old, like candlelight."

"Why candlelight?" the neighborhood boy asked.

"It is much better than darkness!" his classmate replied.

As I write this story, I'm thinking of my editor and friend, Dr. Henry Felson, who's now almost ninety years old and is still a voracious reader and wonderful conversationalist. Even though Dr. Felson has become frail with age, he yet remains a beacon of love to those who know him.

Grinding Needles

62. Grinding Needles

It was a beautiful spring day, with birds singing and flowers blossoming everywhere. A schoolboy, unable to resist temptation, sneaked out of his classroom, murmuring to himself, "Nothing is more difficult than reading and writing. It just requires too much effort to try to remember the lessons. I would rather play."

The boy forgot his studies entirely as he ran through fields of wildflowers and waded across mountain streams. When he passed a remote village, he saw an old woman busily grinding an iron rod.

"What are you doing with that rod, dear old lady?" the student asked.

"I am grinding this iron rod into a needle," the old lady replied, without stopping her work.

The student laughed and asked teasingly, "Tell me, wise lady, what is your secret for grinding this huge rod into a tiny needle?"

"Persistence is the key, my son," replied the woman who continued to work.

Just when the student thought she was joking, he discovered a recently ground needle nearby. He now realized how foolish he had been for regarding studying as the hardest thing in the world.

Inspired by the old woman, the student returned to school and studied diligently thereafter.

Though it may not be our goal to grind needles, all great achievements stem from an attitude that is dogged to a degree of foolishness.

63. Training a Cock

Once an old master gave his student a chick and told him to raise it to be a fighting cock. "When it is ready, come to see me," the master said.

The student bowed to his master and left. From that day onward the student took very good care of this chick, making sure it had plenty of exercise and food. As a result, the cock grew bigger and stronger than any chicken he had ever seen. Now the cock seemed to be ready and the student brought it to see his master.

"Master, I have followed your instruction to raise the chick to be a fighting cock. Do you think it is ready now?" The student showed his big bird to his teacher.

"Not yet," replied his master. "It has no fighting experience."

So the student began to train his bird to fight with other cocks. When he could not find another cock matching its skill and courage, he went to see his teacher.

"Master, I have trained this cock to fight like no other, surely it is ready for the prize fight."

"Not yet," replied his master. "It is too eager to fight."

After ten days the student brought the cock to his master and said, "Master, the cock has learned to mellow its temper. Do you think it is ready now?"

"Not yet," replied the master. "It is too proud."

Then one day the master came by his student's place and saw his student's fighting cock staring into the empty air like a wooden bird. He proclaimed, "Now it is ready."

True to his master's words, the student's impassive bird scared away all challengers and became a champion.

We can learn from the process of training a cock. Confucius once said, "One does not become a real person until one reaches the age of thirty." Thirty years of life in Confucius's time is probably equivalent to forty or fifty in our time.

Young people are in a learning period and have no real life experience. Once they enter into society, they are eager to prove their abilities and make many mistakes. As life goes on, they gain some victories along the way and many become proud just like the fighting bird. By the time they reach mid-life, they will have experienced many defeats and triumphs. Some of them will begin to understand that life is more than what it appears and, looking beyond the complexity of life, become "real persons."

Of course, many of us never complete our training process and remain too eager to fight or too proud to know our limitations.

Throwing a Child into Water

64. Throwing a Child into Water

A long time ago, a traveler was walking along a riverbank when he came upon a woman carrying a young boy on her back. The traveler watched in amazement as the woman hurriedly untied her child, now crying loudly, and attempted to cast him into the river. Rushing forward, the traveler asked, "Why are you trying to throw your child into the river, woman? Can't you see that he is afraid? After all, he is only a child. Let him go!"

"We need to cross this river and there are no boats available," the woman replied.

"The child will certainly drown in these deep waters, woman. Can't you see he is trembling with fear?" admonished the traveler.

"Dear sir, thank you for your concern. But please don't be fooled by his disobedience. He will swim like a fish once he is in the water."

"How can you be so sure, woman?" the traveler asked.

"Because his father is a good swimmer," the woman replied proudly.

Many of us tend to forget that human skills are a consequence of hard work, not inborn mechanisms. It is always easier to blame our failures on a lack of family background than to continue trying.

Remember the proverb: generals and prime ministers are not born of a special breed; anyone can reach a high position if one tries hard enough.

Playing Music to Buffalos

65. Playing Music to Buffalos

A certain musician was born and reared in a city and seldom went to the countryside. Once, when he was invited to a country home, the musician brought his instrument with him in order to perform for his host; but the country people were too busy to listen to his music.

Since he saw many water buffalos lying in the field doing nothing, the musician thought, Why not perform for the buffalos? So he decided to sit in front of them and play his favorite music. The music was so beautiful that even the musician himself was moved to tears. But when he took a peep at his audience, he was dismayed to find the buffalos oblivious to what he was playing.

Seeing that his audience was not interested, the musician grew disheartened. But just as he was about to leave, a mosquito flew past his nose. Suddenly inspired, he thought, Why not change the music? With his instrument he began to create some noises resembling mosquitos and flies. Furthermore, when he imitated a lost calf's call for help, many buffalos stood up eagerly and began to move their tails. A satisfied smile came to the musician's face as he finally received a standing ovation!

Music and words have different effects on different people. Do you remember the last time you became frustrated when someone refused to listen to you? Next time instead of getting frustrated, why not change the music?

66. A Charging Bull's Tail

A rich man was fond of showing off his paintings to his guests. On one occasion, the man pointed to his favorite painting, commenting "This painting of a charging bull is the most realistic one I've ever seen. Look at the sharp horns and fuming nostrils of the bull!" All his friends nodded in agreement.

Just then a buffalo boy entered the house because the rich man had summoned him to run an errand. When the boy saw the picture he laughed.

"Why are you laughing, my boy? Don't you know anything about painting?" the man asked, fuming.

"My landlord, I know nothing about painting, but I do know something about bulls," replied the buffalo boy. "When a bull is charging its tail is tucked in tight. But in your picture, the charging bull has its tail stuck out high. How could it have strength?"

The rich man was embarrassed and never again bragged about his painting.

Confucius says, "Among every three people, there must be a teacher for me."

If we are as humble as Confucius, we can gain a lot of knowledge from others. For instance, a buffalo boy, though low in social status, can teach us about bulls; a weaver can teach us about weaving; a plumber can teach us about pipes.

67. A Skillful Dragon Butcher

"Learn to fix furniture?" A rich young man laughed at his poor playmate. "I have set a higher goal than that: I want to become a dragon butcher."

Three years later, the poor playmate had learned a trade which enabled him to support his family while the rich young man, investing all his family treasure, had become a splendid dragon killer. However, the skill of killing dragons was useless because there weren't any dragons to be killed.

One might argue that the dragon butcher could become a teacher. Certainly, today's universities are replete with dragon-butchering courses. There are enough rich young people who are eager to learn anything that is glorious.

But if you had a choice, wouldn't you rather learn something practical than something that's merely theoretical?

68. Talking

There was once a student in a rural school who would talk incessantly whenever his teacher merely asked him a simple question. The teacher advised him to speak concisely and get to the point but the student couldn't understand why. Finally the teacher asked, "What creatures make a lot of noise and yet nobody pays them attention?"

"Crickets and toads," replied the student.

"That's right, my student. Now can you tell me the animal to which everybody pays attention when it makes sounds?"

"The cock, of course. When the cock crows it wakens everybody," replied the student.

"Then would you rather talk ceaselessly like a cricket or a toad, being ever ignored; or would you rather speak succinctly like a cock, commanding attention?" asked the teacher.

The student got the point.

Most of us enjoy talking and loathe listening. Why? Because, while it does not require effort to talk about something we already know, it takes labor, through listening, to learn something new.

From time to time, I've embarrassed myself by talking too much. Once I got on an elevator full of people and pointed to two blond kids near me, commenting to a man with dark hair, "Their father must have blond hair!"

"I am their father!" the man replied irritably.

I kept quiet the rest of the elevator ride.

69. A Diligent Student

Deep into the night a student studied diligently under a dim light. Wails of pain occasionally came from the student's room, breaking the silence of the night. All his neighbors had grown accustomed to these tortured sounds coming, night after night, from the student's hut.

One day a visitor heard the wails, and, being curious, peeked into the student's room. He saw the student, with his hair bound by a string suspended from above, reading. Each time the student dosed off, the string would pull his hair and the pain would wake him up. Just as the visitor thought he had entirely solved the mystery, the student jumped up with a yell. The student had pressed against a nail on his chair as he leaned back!

To the visitor's admiration, the student was now fully alert and, after adjusting the positions of the string and nail, diligently studying.

Every successful person has his or her own stories to tell, for each has struggled to become a better person.

People don't need to pull their hair or punch their bodies to get ahead, but a spirit of self-sacrifice remains as valid a guiding light for success today as it was thousands of years ago.

70. One-Eyed Net

During the harvesting season there were many sparrows threatening to eat the crops on a small farm. So the landlord asked his servants to do something about the situation.

The servants wove a net and began to catch sparrows with it immediately. Meanwhile, the landlord's only son, who was home from school on vacation, observed the servants with great interest. After he had watched the bird catching for a while, the son went to see his father.

"My father, may I suggest a way to catch sparrows which will save you a lot of money?"

"By all means, my son; I knew you would become an intelligent person on the very day that I sent you to school," the landlord replied.

"Thank you, my father." The son began, "In catching sparrows, is it true that each bird is caught by only one of the many eyes in the net?"

"Yes, that is very true, my son." The landlord was pleased with his son's observation.

"Well, if it is true that only one eye is needed to catch a bird, what is the use of the rest of the eyes in the net? Aren't they a waste of money? From now on, I suggest you should ask your servants to weave one-eyed nets only."

The landlord was shocked by his son's stupidity.

In bird catching, no one knows which eye of the net will trap a bird. If you regard all but one eye as a waste of money, you will not catch even a single bird.

Similarly, in achieving goals, no one knows on which try you will accomplish your goal. If you only try once, you can hardly become successful. Seemingly fruitless trials are just as integral to the process of achievement as eyes are to a net.

71. Concentration

"Master, why is it that one of my sons is a good chess player while the other is not? Is one of my sons more intelligent than the other?" a mother asked her son's chess teacher.

Instead of answering the question immediately, the teacher led the mother to the school yard where her sons were playing chess. While one of the sons was concentrating on the game, the other was looking up at some geese which happened to be flying by.

"You see, the one who puts his mind into playing chess is the one who masters the art. The other, though as intelligent as the first, fails to learn the art because his mind is on something else. Concentration, good lady, sets your sons apart as success and failure, not intelligence."

I recently had two young Tai Chi students, a pair of ten-year-old girls who are identical twins. They looked so alike that I couldn't tell them apart at first. Gradually, however, I learned to recognize the twins by the way they practiced Tai Chi: one took it seriously while the other did not. Naturally, the more serious girl became a much better practitioner than her twin.

Why does one identical twin concentrate on Tai Chi while the other does not? Although I don't have an answer, one thing is obvious -- heredity has nothing to do with it. Success truly depends on the individual.

72. Habit

"When I was young," a teacher lectured to his students on the subject of habit, "I used to study in a room with a shallow hole in its floor. Although each time I paced the floor my feet tread on this hole, in time I learned to ignore it.

"Then one day my father, when he saw the depression in my room, laughed and said, 'If you can't take care of one room, how can you take care of a nation?' Immediately, he ordered a servant to fill the hole.

"The next time I paced the floor, when I reached the area where the hole had been, I felt as if the floor had been raised!"

The teacher sighed and continued, "My habit of ignoring the hole had distorted my judgment: I had accepted a floor which was bad for my feet as being normal!"

A proverb says: one becomes red when one is near red dye and black when near black dye. Shouldn't we be careful in choosing our friends and environment?

Part Seven:

Procrastination
& Action

推遲與行動

Waiting for a Rabbit

73. Waiting for a Rabbit

In a remote area, there lived an old farmer and his son. The farmer was getting old and relied on his son for farming and hunting.

One day during the hunting season the son went hunting and came back with a huge rabbit. But then for many days thereafter he failed to bring home a single animal, not even a squirrel, and the father became anxious. "My son, when I was young I brought home many game animals. What has happened to them now? Have they all gone -- not even a bird or two left?"

"Be patient, father, be patient. I will get them," replied the son.

As the son continued to come home empty-handed for many more days, the father resolved to follow his son secretly. The farmer was greatly disappointed to see his son sitting quietly underneath a tree on the hunting grounds.

"Why are you sitting here and not doing anything, my son?" the farmer confronted his son.

"My father, I am not just sitting here. I am waiting for a rabbit to hit this tree," the son pointed to the tree trunk where he was leaning. "Remember the rabbit I brought home? I found the rabbit right here after it ran and hit this tree. Be patient, father, be patient. I will get them."

The old farmer was much dismayed by his son's stupidity.

As was the case when the rabbit struck the tree, success sometimes comes easily to us when we are in the right place at the right time. But such random success is a blessing only if we realize it happens haphazardly. If not, such a success can mislead us into valuing pure luck over hard work.

Marking a Boat to Retrieve a Sword

74. Marking a Boat to Retrieve a Sword

"I have dropped my sword into the water. Stop the boat, stop the boat," a passenger cried softly to himself as the ferry sailed on. Even though he realized that any opportunity to recover his sword was limited to this moment, he was too timid to ask for help. How inconvenient to stop a boat in the middle of the lake and start again! he thought. It is just too troublesome.

Convinced that he shouldn't act now, the passenger made a mark on the boat at the site where he had lost his precious sword. "Once the boat reaches its destination, I'll jump into the water to retrieve my sword," the passenger comforted himself and waited.

As the boat traveled far from where he had originally dropped his sword, the passenger lost his opportunity forever.

Each of us is a boat sailing along on our life journey. To drift from day to day is convenient; to stop our routine and go after unforeseen opportunities is not. How many marks have you carved on your boats to remind yourself to do this or that and then never accomplished them? Unless you stop and act now, your boat will be covered with empty marks when you finally reach your destination.

75. Fireflies and Snow

"My students," a teacher told his class, "once there were two young scholars whose families could not afford burning oil. To provide light for their studies at night, one of them placed many fireflies in a jar, creating a makeshift lamp, while the other used snow to reflect moonlight for his study."

After hearing this story, the students became motivated to study hard and their teacher was very pleased. When the teacher heard that one of his students was actually studying with fireflies, he visited the student in order to give him some encouragement. The teacher was surprised, however, to learn that his student was not at home studying.

"Where has my student gone?" asked the teacher.

"Since early morning, my son has been catching fireflies in the woods," replied the student's mother.

The teacher then went to see another student, who had reportedly been using snow to reflect light for his study. Reaching the student's house, the teacher was surprised to find the student staring at the sky instead of studying and lamenting that it wasn't going to snow.

The students confused the use of fireflies and snow with the act of diligently learning.

Some of us, at one time or the other, behave just like the students. I used to mistakenly regard working late at the office as being a sign of hard work. Eager to label myself an industrious worker, I stayed late every day to do work, which, if I hadn't wanted to stay late, I easily could have finished during the day.

76. Lost a Goat

Once a farmer discovered that some of his goats had disappeared, and later realized that his sons were to blame for the loss.

"How many goats have you lost?" yelled the farmer, as he brandished a whip and glared at the older of his two sons, both of whom were kneeling before him.

"One," replied the elder son.

"Where were you when the goat ran away?" the farmer asked sternly. With his eyes cast on the floor, the elder son admitted he was gambling at the time.

"Gambling!" thundered the farmer, whipping his son hard.

"You," said the farmer, turning to the younger son. "How many goats have you lost?"

"Just one," replied the younger son.

"What is your excuse for losing *just one*?"

"I was studying, father!" the son replied righteously.

"So what?" said the farmer, whipping the younger son equally hard. "Even though your cause was nobler, it's still no excuse for neglecting your job!"

Excuses, excuses, and excuses; there are always plenty of them. More often than not, we can come up with a "noble" cause which will excuse us from our present tasks. So let us be aware of our own excuses, for otherwise we will not be reliable people.

77. A Poor Person

On a moonless night a thief broke into a poor man's house instead of a rich man's house as he had intended. The thief found this household was so poor and dirty that there wasn't anything worth taking -- even the pots and pans were covered with dirt. However, just as the thief was beginning to feel sorry for the residents of this house, he heard someone inside the bedroom yawning.

When the thief tiptoed to the front door, he heard a man request sleepily, "Please help me close the door." The thief shook his head because he knew why the man was so poor.

Laziness is a major cause of poverty in developed nations. When I was a student, I bought a third-rate automobile with money I earned as a busboy. I felt pity toward those without cars and would occasionally pick up hitchhikers. When, however, on one particular occasion a hitchhiker asked me for a dollar, it suddenly occurred to me that the only difference between that guy and me was that I worked and he didn't (at that time restaurants were desperate for busboys). I never picked up a hitchhiker again.

78. A Wooden Pole for a Bed

Once a carpenter asked his apprentice, "We need strong upright lumber for the house beam. Go to the forest and cut a tree for that purpose!"

"Will do, Master," the apprentice replied, leaving for the forest. Soon he brought back a very sturdy and straight tree trunk.

"Well done, Student," the master applauded. "By the way, our customer has a bed with only three poles, and he needs a fourth one. Would you please go to the forest and find a tree for it?"

"That's easy, Master. I'll bring one back in no time!" the apprentice boasted as he left. However, he came back only after a long period of time.

"Where is the tree?" the master demanded.

"Master, I searched the entire mountain, but couldn't locate a single tree that grows downward. So I returned empty-handed," the student, with his head down, replied.

The apprentice was thinking too much about a simple task. While it's true that a house beam goes up and a bed pole goes down, the trees used to construct them don't have to match these directions.

If you are often unable to finish simple tasks, perhaps you, like the apprentice, are regarding things as more complicated than they actually are.

79. First Drum

Two rival armies were ready to engage each other on an open battlefield. Soldiers on both sides were in high spirits, waiting for the signal to attack. It was customary that when one army hit their drums the other side would follow suit, advancing to engage the other in battle. So as the soldiers of one army first heard the drums, they raised their shields, waved their swords and readied themselves for war.

But this time there was no response from the other army, and so the general ordered his men to hit their drums again.

"My advisor, shouldn't we strike our drums now?" asked the prince of the other army impatiently.

"Not yet," replied the advisor.

It was only when the opposing army hit their drums for the third time that the advisor said calmly, "Now hit the drums and advance!"

Following his advisor's words, the prince gave the order to attack. How quickly his soldiers defeated the enemy!

After winning the battle, the prince asked his advisor, "Why did we wait for the third wave of drums to attack?"

"You see, my Prince, fighting involves both the mind and the body. During the first wave of drums, a soldier's blood runs high, blocking his fear of death. This is the best time to engage in battle. On the other hand, if the soldiers have time to think, their courage will evaporate as doubts creep into their minds. So we won the battle because our soldiers were fearless, having heard only one wave of drums. On the other hand, our enemies had their minds opened to the possibility of defeat as they waited for third wave of drums," replied the advisor.

The prince nodded.

Do you want to accomplish more goals in your life? The recipe is simple: just plunge into battle each time you hear your own inner first wave of drums calling yourself to action. If you wait for the second and the third drums, your mind will have time to envision real and imaginary obstacles, which inevitably leads to paralysis and failure.

80. A King Dismissed His Administrator

One day a king stunned everyone by dismissing a very high-ranking official without any obvious reason.

"Why did you discharge our Administrator, my dear King?" the queen asked privately. "I never heard any criticism directed against him during the three years he spent with us."

"That's the very reason I released him, my dear Queen," the king replied.

The king understood that there will always be opposition to any course of action taken by an administrator. A lack of criticism necessarily implies that no actions have been taken. Why should the king continue to employ someone who has never done anything?

So if you have many critics, congratulations, for you are doing something worthy of opposition. But if, on the other hand, you are attracting no criticism from anyone, beware, for you may be wasting the opportunity of a lifetime.

81. Sinking Boats and Breaking Woks

An army had just crossed the river into enemy territory. Instead of allowing the soldiers to start camp fires, the general ordered them to sink the boats and break the woks.

"Are you sure, my general?" cautioned his senior advisor. "What if our enemies are too strong for us? We will have cut off our means of retreat. And if we don't overcome our enemies in time, we will have nothing to eat!"

"My advisor, there are no 'what if's' in front of us--only life and death. This is war, not a game," replied the general, proceeding with his order.

At first the soldiers were horrified when they realized that all floating vessels and cooking utensils were destroyed. But once they realized they were in a position of no retreat, their survival instinct took over and their minds focused on only one thought--advance.

Facing a choice between death and advance, the soldiers fought gallantly and defeated their enemies.

If we only try halfheartedly to achieve what we want in life, our possibility of success is small. Why? Because each time we encounter an obstacle the thought "I can't do it" will appear, causing us to scramble for our own inner boat and cooking wok.

On the other hand, if we affirm "I can do it" then our mind and body will act as one, giving us the power of concentration to climb even the highest mountains.

Part Eight:

Anger, Worry, Greed

Shadow of a Snake

82. Shadow of a Snake

Once a hunter invited his friend over for a drink. After one glass of wine, the friend became visibly nervous and left the party early.

When the hunter saw his friend a few days later he asked, "What has happened to you, my friend? You look so tired and worried."

"I don't know why, but ever since I drank your glass of wine, I can hardly eat or sleep. I think I am going to die," his friend replied.

After returning home, the hunter poured wine into the same glass used by his friend and was puzzled to see an image of a snake appearing inside the glass. But when he turned the glass to another angle the snake disappeared. He smiled as he realized that the "snake" was merely a reflection of his bow hanging on the wall.

The hunter invited his friend back and recreated the scene. His friend sighed with relief when he understood that he had not eaten a snake and hence was not going to die.

Once the friend understood the source of his snake, he began to eat and sleep as before.

The man in the above story was lucky because the hunter was able to pinpoint the origin of his "snake." But many of us are not so lucky. Most of the snakes we have drunk, even though long forgotten or suppressed by our conscious mind, are alive and well in our subconscious.

The next time you wake up in the middle of the night feeling depressed or helpless without knowing why, recognize that "snakes" have emerged to haunt you. Relax and go back to sleep, for they are not real.

83. A Bad-Tempered Fish

A fish with a quick temper was swimming in such a hurry that it hit a tree stump. Instantly, the fish became so angry that air got into its body. Like a balloon being filled up with air, the enraged fish was helplessly buoyed up to the surface. An eagle flew by and snatched this helpless fish for a meal.

Anger cost the fish its life. This can happen to us too. When we get angry, the blood goes to our head and we are ready to explode. Thus we put ourselves in a vulnerable position for illness or even death to attack.

84. A Tiger Walked Away

Once upon a time, a family lived in a mountainous region where there were many tigers. On one occasion, the housewife went with her two young sons to a nearby river to wash clothes. When a tiger appeared, the housewife jumped into the river to take cover. However, the two sons were busily playing in the sand, oblivious to the danger.

The tiger stalked cautiously toward its prey. But instead of running, the children showed no fear toward the tiger. Confused, the tiger tried to scare the children by brushing its head against them, but to no avail. Sensing no fear or reaction from the children, the tiger was unable to muster its usual power. Consequently, it walked away, leaving the children unharmed.

Can this story be true? Have you seen documentary films on snake trainers kissing venomous cobras or divers petting man-eating sharks? These films have shown us that people can avoid harm if they relax and remain calm when dealing with deadly subjects.

Maybe you can also adopt a calm attitude in dealing with your daily stress, thereby minimizing its harmful effects.

Healing a Hump

85. Healing a Hump

A man went to see a healer about his back. Though the man would have been six feet tall, he was a hunchback and stood only four feet above the ground. Although the infirmity could have been healed at an earlier age, the man had previously been unable to afford medical treatment.

The healer was indeed glad to see a deformed patient entering with a sack of gold.

"Doctor, if you can heal my back this gold will be yours," said the man, putting the gold on a table.

"I have healed many hunchbacks before and I can heal you in no time," replied the healer, as he took the gold and signaled his patient to lay on the ground with his hump up.

"Ah!" the patient yelled in tears as the healer jumped on his back. "Are you trying to kill me?" he asked in alarm.

"Please don't ask any questions. Let me take care of your back!" replied the healer as he readied himself to jump again.

The hunchback crawled to his feet and fled.

The healer saw only the gold and the hump, but not the man who had them.

I have read that many unnecessary surgeries are performed every year in the United States. I won't try to explain why this happens, but if I had a hump and a lot of money, I would be very careful.

86. A Fish Tail

Once a fish and an old frog lived together harmoniously as neighbors and friends. One day it was rumored that the ruler of the sea had ordered all creatures with tails beheaded. The fish was terrified and swam to his old friend for comfort. But when the fish reached the old frog's place, he was surprised to find the old frog shivering with fear.

"Mr. Frog, what has happened to you? Why are you so frightened?" asked the fish.

"Haven't you heard that our ruler is going to kill all tailed creatures?" said the frog.

"My dear friend, you don't even have a tail. Why do you worry yourself so?" the fish asked.

"But when I was a young tadpole, I, too, had a tail," answered the old frog, continuing to shake like a leaf.

We all have our own childhood "tails" which haunt us from time to time. But since these "tails" are in the past, why should our present be preoccupied by them?

87. Taking a Cow as Punishment

A man once discovered his cow in a neighbor's barn, so he confronted the neighbor, "Why did you take my cow?"

"Your cow trespassed into my cornfield and ate most of my crop. Don't you realize that this was a crime? That's why I took your cow," said the neighbor self-righteously.

"But my cow is worth much more than your corn," responded the man. "You most certainly are in the wrong."

"Even though your cow appears to cost more, when you consider that each grain of my corn could have generated hundreds of grains which would, in turn, have given thousands and thousands of grains, it actually does not. It is really worth much more than your cow," said the neighbor.

The man left unhappily and waited for his neighbor's cow to, in turn, stray into his field.

Of course, the punishment of taking a cow did not fit the crime of trespassing. But this story is not talking about judgments based on facts. It addresses how we judge ourselves based on conjectures. Sometimes, the punishment we render to ourselves is much more severe than the crime deserves.

One day a good friend of mine told me, "Luke, I am going to tell you something which I have never told anyone before, not even my wife. (I forget what had triggered my physician friend to suddenly pour out his secret to me.) "When I was young," my friend began, "I drew some graffiti on a wall. Since I was a 'nice' boy no one suspected me. But the boy next door was known for being naughty, and he was punished for my crime. I felt very bad. Years later, I finally got enough courage to apologize to the boy for what I had done. Though he had no recollection of the incident, I couldn't stop feeling guilty about it."

To a naughty boy, drawing graffiti is common. But to a nice boy, disfiguring a wall and not being punished for it is a crime for which he'll be punished for the rest of his life.

A Buffalo Boy Finds a Gold Nugget

88. A Buffalo Boy Finds a Gold Nugget

Every morning a buffalo boy ate some yam and soup with rice, donned his worn-out clothes and hat, took out his bamboo flute, and left to tend his cattle. Whether it was winter, spring, summer or fall, the buffalo tender was always delighted with nature. He sang and played the flute among birds and wildflowers in the springtime and nestled meditatively near a still pond during winter. The boy was free and happy and the water buffalos he tended were strong and tame.

Then one day the buffalo boy came across a gold nugget near the road to the grassland. He could hardly believe his good luck as he bent to pick up the nugget from the ground. Seeing no one nearby, he secured the newfound treasure in his pocket.

From that day onward, the boy was preoccupied with his gold nugget and had no time for anything else. He sang less and less, and no long played his flute. He was oblivious to the songs of birds, the color of wildflowers, and the soothing sound of running water. His buffalos became thin and unmanageable.

The gold nugget had become the buffalo boy's obsession.

By gaining something valuable, the boy had lost his appreciation for life. Indeed, material gains can easily cause us to lose our childlike love of nature and joy in life.

89. Adding Legs to a Snake

"Let's share it!" suggested one of three servants after they had received a glass of wine from their landlord.

"This glass of wine is not enough for three persons; we should find a way to determine who of us will drink it," countered another servant.

"How about drawing a snake?" the third servant suggested. "And whoever completes his snake first gets the drink. What do you think, my friends?"

The other two knew the third servant was a quick painter, but couldn't come up with a better idea. So they prepared paper and brushes and began their drawings.

The third servant finished his drawing well ahead of the other two. But just as he seized the glass and was about to drink he thought, Well, I am so much ahead of my friends that I have plenty of time to be creative. Consequently, the third servant took up his brush again and added four legs to his snake.

When the next servant finished his drawing, he took the glass from his peer and drank the wine.

"Why did you drink the wine when I was the one who first finished drawing?" the servant cried.

"I have never seen a snake with legs!" replied the other.

Often people become careless and make mistakes once they think that victory is in hand.

Once it was reported that a man suspected of committing a robbery was being questioned by the police. The man, who had answered every question to the officers' satisfaction, thought he had covered his crime perfectly. But just before the police were about to let him go, he became talkative and remarked, "I had a mask on, how could anyone possibly identify me?"

90. Wishing a Thief

"Who's there?" a man awakened by a noise in the middle of the night asked. A thief was startled and fled, leaving a stolen coat in the house.

The man got of out of bed and inspected his residence. When he found an expensive coat lying on the floor, he was delighted. From that time onward, he left his doors open every night, hoping another thief would enter.

This man was only thinking of the unintended fortune left by the thief instead of the potential danger of letting a thief into his house.

I remember more than one occasion in my childhood when I wished I were sick so as to get attention from adults. Recently, I suspected an aged relative of mine of desiring to be sick so he would get more attention from his children. Unfortunately, his wish became reality and his illness almost killed him.

91. Gain Little, Lose Big

A long time ago, a king whose kingdom was surrounded by treacherous mountains was proud of the fact that none of his enemies could reach him. Then one day, the ruler of a neighboring nation sent word that he wanted to present the king with a gold-producing bull; all the king needed to do was to open a road to get it.

Although the king was wary of the intentions of his counterpart, he was unwilling to dismiss this offer easily. So he sent a scout to investigate his neighbor's gift. His neighbor, however, anticipated this move and placed a mysteriously decorated stone bull with a few gold chips along a mountainside path.

Upon hearing the scout's report, the king was pleased, and ordered his men to open a road to bring in the bull.

As the king moved the stone bull to his land, his neighbor's army, using the same route as the bull, followed. By gaining a stone bull, the king lost a kingdom!

When greed blinds our vision, we can lose much.

In a midwestern city, it was reported that a young robber once held up a convenient store with a gun. When the burglar alarm went off, the young man ran away with a few hundred dollars, but left his gun in the store. Later the police found that the gun was a collector's item worth more than ten thousand dollars!

Part Nine:

Life

Blessings in Disguise

92. Blessings in Disguise

"Why are you so depressed and neglectful of your work, my young neighbor?" asked an old man when he saw his friend sobbing.

"I have just lost my horse, my good neighbor. Without my horse, it is hard for me to make a living," replied the dejected young man.

"Be cheerful, my neighbor. I have lived long enough to know that seemingly bad luck may actually prove a blessing in time," consoled the old man.

A few days later the lost horse returned home with a group of mustangs. The young man was elated and came to thank his neighbor. But the old man cautioned him, "Don't be overjoyed, my neighbor. It might prove bad luck in time."

The young man, though puzzled, was too busy dealing with his new fortune to think about his neighbor's warning. Soon he fell from one of his new horses as he was trying to tame it and broke his leg. The young man again became dejected.

"Don't be sad, my young neighbor. Your broken leg may prove a blessing in time," the old man comforted his friend.

True to his neighbor's words, the young man was spared from being drafted into a doomed campaign because of his broken leg.

Hard times come and go and so does fortune. Life is like a game where sometimes you win and sometimes you lose, and players don't count their earnings until the game is over. So don't sum up your life's worth while you are still in the game of life. Colonel Sanders didn't become a millionaire until the age of sixty-five!

93. Soft and Hard

Sitting on his grandfather's lap, a child asked, "Grandpa, people say that you are wise. Can you tell me something about life?"

Instead of answering the question directly, the grandfather grimaced like a monkey, showing his toothless gums.

"Where are your teeth, grandpa?" the child teased.

Then the grandfather protruded his tongue like a clown, causing the child to laugh heartily.

The next day, the mother asked her son what he had learned from his grandfather.

"Nothing. He merely showed me his toothless gums and his tongue," replied the son as he left to play.

The mother pondered a while, and then smiled as she realized what her father was trying to teach her child: life, in general, behaves in the same fashion as that of her father's teeth and tongue. Her father's teeth were lost because they were hard; his tongue still remained because it was soft.

Why do people perform better in sports when they are relaxed?

Why do people feel drained when they have hard feelings against others and feel energetic when they are loving?

Perhaps softness is indeed, better than hardness.

94. Marriage

In the moonlight, a young scholar saw an old man paging through a thick book. Being curious, the scholar asked, "What are you reading, sir?"

The old man looked up and replied, "This is the holy *Marriage Book* in which all past and future married couples' names are written."

"What do you mean by 'past and future couples', sir?" the young scholar asked.

"If two people are bound by this string," said the old man, holding up a red string, "they will become husband and wife, regardless of time."

"Sir, you are joking, aren't you?"

"Marriage is a serious thing, young scholar. It is not a joking matter," the old man replied. He then pointed to two people who were walking by, a young girl accompanied by a blind woman, and stated, "This girl will be your future wife." And so saying, the old man left the bewildered young man, disappearing into the night. But suddenly to the scholar's horror, a crazy man waving a sharp knife slashed the little girl's forehead. With blood dripping down her face, she fell to the ground and cried for help. However, the young scholar was disgusted at the thought of marrying a blind woman's daughter, so he walked away without helping her.

Fourteen years later the young scholar, who was now a high-ranking official, married the beautiful daughter of a wealthy family. On the wedding night, he discovered that his bride had a small scar on her forehead. Then she told him about what had happened one night fourteen years ago, when someone tried to kill her while she was on her way home with her blind nanny.

The husband kissed his bride's forehead and left her temporarily. Alone, he entered the backyard, knelt down, and promised silently to the moon that he would never leave his wife again.

The couple lived happily ever after.

Are our marriages fixed before we even know it? If so, who fixes them? Judging by the number of people who are unhappy with their marriages, whoever is in charge must be someone like the old man -- reading couples' names with dull eyes, under dim moonlight!

On the other hand, if we consider our marriages as happening by pure chance, then it must give us pause. Maybe our marriages are not ideal, but aren't they still special when the chance of two particular persons coming together as husband and wife in this lifetime is one in many billions?

95. Free in Water

Once, there was a pond in which lived many fish. All of the fish lived freely, without much interaction among themselves. Then during one prolonged dry season, when the water was almost completely evaporated, the fish found themselves gasping for air.

As the weather remained dry, the fish were in a desperate situation until a wise fish suggested that they help each other by secreting saliva into each other's gills. As time went on, the fish became more and more dependent on each other for living. A young fish commented, "I can't imagine the kind of life we fish were leading in the days before we began serving and caring for each other."

When an old fish heard the comment, he shook his head and murmured to himself, "I would rather swim freely in the water without paying much attention to the others."

The young fish, who had not tasted freedom, thought the artificial way of helping each other was best. Yet for the old fish, freedom was supreme.

By the same token, if we were to clear away all the rain forests, the natives of these regions, who have been living freely among the trees, would discover our "civilized" way of life. Of course, some of the young natives would thank us for rescuing them from the Stone Age. But for the old, their harmonious way of living together in nature would be gone forever. Shouldn't we leave them alone?

Incidental Victims

96 . Incidental Victims

The king's guards were in hot pursuit of a thief who had stolen the king's crown jewel. In a hurry, the thief threw the jewel into a nearby pond and disappeared into the forest. Although some of the guards jumped into the water to retrieve the jewel, none could find it.

When the king learned that his favorite jewel was lost in a pond, he ordered the water removed so the bottom could be thoroughly searched.

Naturally, the fish, which had lived harmoniously in the pond for centuries, dried up and died.

In a similar fashion, when governments allow tropical forests to be cut for timber and land, indigenous peoples who have been living in these forests peacefully for centuries become incidental victims.

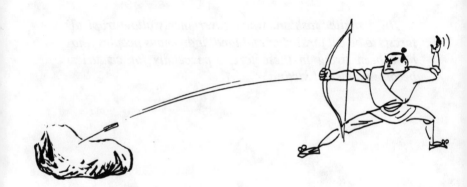

The Power of Belief

97. The Power of Belief

Once as a hunter ventured into the woods at night, he came across a figure resembling a tiger lying in his path, and he shot an arrow at it with all his might.

The next morning, when the hunter went out to claim his trophy, he discovered to his surprise that his arrow was deeply imbedded in a rock. When he tried to repeat his feat, his arrow scarcely made a dent on the surface of the stone. The hunter was baffled at first. Then it dawned on him that during the night, he so regarded the rock as a tiger that he believed it was penetrable and it was. But during the day, he saw the rock as a rock; and, not believing he could penetrate a rock, so lost his magical power.

Is this story believable? Is it possible for a mother, who can ordinarily scarcely lift a hundred-pound object to lift a car, weighing thousands of pounds, just to save her child? We can accomplish amazing things if we have faith.

Perhaps the next time you encounter an obstacle, instead of seeing it as an impenetrable rock, you should regard it as merely a sleeping beast and so overcome it with one mighty thrust!

98. A Secret Remedy

A family whose trade was color dying had a secret remedy for treating hands which were bleeding after exposure to bitterly cold water. For generations, the family had kept this secret method to themselves. But one day a scholar who had heard of the remedy offered the family one hundred gold nuggets for the formula.

The family members were elated because, even though they had benefited from the formula to the extent of being able to keep their business running during winter, their income had never amounted to much.

After obtaining the formula, the scholar went to see the king. He offered the preventive to the king's navy, which was currently engaged in frequent winter sea battles. The medicine proved to be very effective in preventing bleeding, and as a direct result of having healthier hands, the king's navy was victorious.

Overjoyed, the king rewarded the scholar with a large piece of land and ten thousand gold nuggets.

The same potion, when applied to different uses, produced different rewards.

Many family medicinal secrets are not being recognized and will inevitably become lost.

Our old friend, "Snake King," tells a story about how his daughter was once bitten by a poisonous snake and sent to a hospital. When he saw his daughter's foot swelling as big as an elephant's, he applied some of his home remedy. The swelling soon disappeared, but when the nurse saw the girl's foot covered with some strange dark lotion, she cursed the father for meddling with the "healing." Because the remedy lacked "scientific evidence" it was never widely used.

99. A Bowl of Rice

Late at night as people were sleeping peacefully in a small remote village, all the dogs started to bark. An old widow was awakened and got up to investigate the noises outside. Opening the front door, she saw a young traveler lying down on her doorstep, exhausted and starving.

The old widow helped the young traveler into her house and gave him a bowl of rice.

"Thank you, gentle woman, I'll never forget your kindness," said the young traveler before he fell soundly asleep.

The next morning, the young traveler woke up early and continued on his journey.

Then one day a few years later, the dogs again barked loudly. The old widow opened her door and found a young high-ranking official at her door. The young official knelt down in front of the old widow and said, "Kind woman, I have come to pay for the bowl of rice you once fed me." Then he signaled his assistants to carry a thousand gold nuggets to her house.

"Thank you for your gift, young traveler, but it was only a bowl of rice that I fed you."

"Yes, it was only a bowl of rice, my dear kind woman, but for me, at the time when I was no better than a beggar, it was worth more than a thousand gold nuggets!"

Good deeds come in circles; as we treat others with kindness and gentleness, so shall good things come back to us in one form or another.

When my mother died, my grandaunt became guardian to my siblings and me, and we lived in her house for many years. Even though it was convenient for her at the time to be so, for us, being motherless, her act of charity was worth a thousand gold nuggets. Every year since we started working, my brother and I have been sending our great-aunt some money. It is not our intent to measure her kindness monetarily, but merely to acknowledge the timelessness of her good deed to my family.

The Unseen Ghost

100. The Unseen Ghost

Once upon a time, the high priest of a religious order interviewed an artist famous for his paintings of horses regarding a commission to paint the walls of his temple. The high priest was an arrogant man, proud of his ability to attract many common people to his temple as worshipers.

Believing that drawing horses would be very easy for someone who had already painted thousands of them during his lifetime, the high priest asked, "Tell me, my son, is it easier to draw a horse or a ghost?"

Without hesitation, the painter replied, "A ghost, of course."

"Why?" The high priest was offended, for, after all, the subject of ghosts was in his area of expertise and ought to be very difficult for a layman such as the painter to understand.

"Because everybody has seen a horse but nobody has ever seen a ghost," replied the painter.

The high priest was at a loss for words.

Is it easier to set up a school or to build a temple? If you wonder why there are more churches in your city than shelters for the homeless, perhaps this story will provide some explanation.

101. A Perfect Life

A poor scholar was sitting alone at the corner table of an inn. He had stopped here while on his way home after having failed an examination. The scholar knew he would now never have a prestigious official job or marry the girl of his dream. So there he sat, reflecting on his misfortune.

A holy man at an adjacent table, hearing the scholar's sighs, felt pity for him and gave him a pillow to rest on. The scholar laid his head on the pillow and, as he fell asleep, he noticed an old lady cooking rice.

As soon as the scholar closed his eyes he dreamed he had passed the examination with high grades. He saw himself becoming a high government official and marrying a beautiful woman. As time went by he had many children, all as healthy and intelligent as himself. At work he was a good official, respected by all his subordinates. At home he was an excellent husband and father and loved by his family. By the time he retired he had money, fame and posterity. After retirement, he took up poetry and painting, two things he had always wanted to pursue. Then he envisioned himself one day suddenly dying of old age. It was then that the poor scholar woke up from his dream.

When he looked up he was surprised to find the old lady still cooking her rice.

Since life, even a perfect one, is still as short as cooking some rice, why should we waste time in wishing for a perfect life?

Fortune comes and goes; so does love. But as life comes, it goes, and is gone. You have already spent much time in pursuing money and love. Isn't it time to pay more attention to the joys of life? Smile when you see the morning sun, smell the scent of the honeysuckle in the summertime, and show a little kindness towards a squirrel in the woods.